TOP 100

taste.COM.AU

THE BIG BOOK OF

Soups

EVERY SOUP
ALL YEAR ROUND

HarperCollins*Publishers*

CONTENTS

HELLO! 6

HOW TO USE THIS BOOK 8

THE SCOOP ON SOUP 11

QUICKER TO LADLE 23

PASTA & NOODLES 77

SLOW & HEARTY 129

VEGIE GOODNESS 179

IMMUNITY BOOSTERS 227

INDEX 247

CREDITS 254

HELLO!

A very big welcome to our *Big Book of Soups* cookbook. Following years of dreaming up and producing all manner of desirable recipes for you to make and enjoy, the Taste team has realised that soups are one of the most coveted of meals but also, funnily enough, one of the most underrated!

Coveted, because soups are undoubtedly delicious, but underrated perhaps because they were once considered boring winter peasant food, made with root vegetables and whatever other produce was at hand.

While grabbing seasonal veg to toss into a soup may still be the norm – there are few meals more wonderful than a hearty pumpkin soup in the middle of July – soups in Australia have taken on a more international flavour in recent decades, giving us much more of a reason to slurp them up at any time of the year.

Take, for example, a clear broth with Asian greens and thin strands of rice noodles, like our Vegetarian Vietnamese pho, p204. It's nice and light for taking a soup spoon to (and the chopsticks!) when the

Keep an eye out for the recipes we've presented as low-cal – there are more than 50! You may be surprised at how tasty and filling they all are – in fact, feel free to eat the whole bowl!

weather is a little warmer. The warmer weather also welcomes quicker soups, when you don't want to slave over a hot stove or heat up the house unnecessarily.

One thing remains the same when it comes to nearly all soups: there really is no fancy prep – just a bit of peeling, slicing and chopping. Keep your knives nice and sharp and you'll soon make quick work of it.

If you're in the chopping mood, why not keep going and make a double batch of your favourite soup? More than half of the recipes in this book can be made and batch-frozen so you can simply reheat and serve them up on a busy evening. You'll find a whole list of freezable soups on page 251. They really are the ideal healthier convenience food.

As soups generally contain a stack of goodness in the form of lean protein, fresh vegies and grains, we've added a sprinkling of information throughout the chapters on the various vitamins and minerals found in our selection of soups, so that you can make healthier choices for you and your family. If you are trying to keep your immune system in top shape, browse our special immunity-boosting soups, from page 227. We've also made a point of highlighting gluten-free soups for those of you are avoiding gluten in your diet, and we have a whole chapter on vegetarian soups (from page 179).

If you now think soups might be the go-to meal of this century, they may also be a great way to shrink your waistline! Keep an eye out for the recipes we've presented as low-cal – there are more than 50! You will be surprised at how tasty and filling they all are – in fact, feel free to eat the whole bowl! :)

Don't worry, we haven't left out your cool-weather favourites. How could we?! You'll find pumpkin soups, chunky minestrones, slow-cooked wonders, and more, all awaiting your eager spoons. Get cooking and enjoy!

Brodee

**BRODEE MYERS,
EDITOR-IN-CHIEF**

HOW TO USE
THE
BIG BOOK
OF SOUPS

Inside this cookbook, you'll find all the recipes and tips you need to create wholesome and satisfying soups for the whole family.

AMAZING FEATURES

Full prep and cooking times

Complete nutrition information

5-star recipe ratings

At-a-glance prep times

Reviews from home cooks

KEY GUIDES
Highlighted dots indicating easy, family friendly, gluten free, low cal, quick and freezable

COOK'S TIPS
Helpful hints and insider knowledge courtesy of our expert food team

COOK'S TIP

See cook's tips for ingredient swaps, make-ahead info and more.

COOK'S TIP

You can use leftover cooked shredded chicken instead of the ham, if you prefer.

CRUNCH THE NUMBERS

Make informed meal choices for you and your family using nutrition panels to help you track your calories and calculate your protein, carbs and fat.

NUTRITION (PER SERVE)

CAL	FAT	SAT FAT	PROTEIN	CARBS
216	7g	2g	14g	18g

INFO AT A GLANCE

Use the icons to find the best choices for you and your family (such as easy, family-friendly, gluten free, low cal, quick and freezable – or all six at once). Just follow the highllghted dots, or turn to our index, which starts on page 247.

● EASY   ● FAMILY-FRIENDLY   ● GLUTEN FREE   ● LOW CAL   ● QUICK   ● FREEZABLE

THE SCOOP ON SOUP

Soups have oodles of benefits. We take you through all basic soup ingredients, nutritional bonuses, and showcase our seasonal favourites. We also have fun with soup bowls and show you how to add a flavour burst using tasty toppers.

THE TASTE.COM.AU GUARANTEE

All taste.com.au recipes are triple-tested, rated and reviewed by Aussie cooks just like you. Plus, every ingredient is as close as your local supermarket.

THE SCOOP ON SOUP

TIPS, TRICKS AND INSPO ON MAKING THE MOST HEALTHY
AND SLURPABLE SOUPS FOR YOU AND YOUR FAMILY.

SUPER BOOST YOUR SOUPS

Delicious, filling and packed with vegetables, soups are an easy, convenient, and often budget-friendly, way to enjoy a nutritious meal.

Not only heavenly to slurp all year round, soups offer a wonderful opportunity to increase your overall intake of protein, vegies, grains and legumes.

We all know a proper intake of vitamins and minerals is essential to maintaining your overall immunity against viruses and other illnesses. Boiling vegies to drain and eat can cause a significant loss of water-soluble vitamins. With soups, however, 70-90 per cent of the water-soluble nutrients in the vegetables are actually retained because the cooking liquid is consumed.

Common soup ingredients, such as root vegetables, grains, legumes and herbs, are not only good for you, but are cost-effective (especially when bought in season), giving soups another reason to frequent the menu. What's more,

dried legumes and grains can be stored for weeks, or even months, in the pantry.

When you're ready to cook, you'll discover that many soups are quick to make, and others can be quickly prepped and popped into a slow cooker or stockpot while you get on with your life. You can even make soups ahead of time, then batch-freeze them for lunches or when you crave a night off cooking.

SOUP STAPLES
Use these tricks to ensure your soups are healthy and packed with flavour.

Flavour base
Any great soup starts with a good stock – as a liquid, powder or cubes. The healthiest are made from natural ingredients, with minimal additives and

reduced sodium. Most commercially available stocks are gluten free, however check the label on cubes/powders.

TRY THIS An easy way to add flavour to a stock is to dissolve miso paste In the liquid (like in our Chicken, miso and ginger soup, p110). For optimal nutrition, add miso towards the end of cooking, as boiling can destroy its probiotic qualities.

Grains, legumes, seeds & nuts
Whole grains and legumes add body and texture to a soup, help you to feel full and act as a natural thickener. They also add dietary fibre, essential for gut health and function, along with prebiotics to help feed your gut microbiome so healthy bacteria can grow and flourish.

Whole grains are also a great source of B vitamins, magnesium, manganese

and phosphorus, while legumes (such as chickpeas, lentils and black beans) are a valuable plant-based source of protein.

Nuts or seeds sprinkled on soups add texture, crunch and healthy fats. **TRY THIS** Add pearl barley, dried red or brown/green lentils and split peas to soups. You can also get a 'soup mix', a combo of beans, lentils and barley. These are all very nutritious, cheap, last for months and taste great!

Add robust whole grains such as barley, freekeh, spelt, farro and brown rice, plus dried pulses, including borlotti beans and lentils, to slow-cooked soups, as they require a longer cooking time. Conversely, add quick-cooking quinoa, couscous and wholemeal pasta, in the last 10-15 minutes of cooking for more speedy soups.

If you're following a gluten-free diet, brown rice, wild rice, quinoa and millet are all gluten-free grains to add to soups, along with legumes including chickpeas,

cannellini beans, lentils and red kidney beans (if using cans, check the label).

Fresh seasonal veg

Soups are a fantastic way to work up to our five-plus serves of vegies a day – a large bowl can easily contain 2-3 serves. Take advantage of vegies in season and they'll be more nutritious and better value for money.

TRY THIS Aim to include at least four different vegies in your soup in a variety of colours. Root vegetables, such as carrots, parsnips and celery, can be added at the start of cooking, while greens such as broccoli, peas and beans, leafy spinach and kale, are best added towards the end so they retain vibrancy. Whole, uncut vegetables, such as sweet potato, pumpkin, potato and onion, are ideal in soups all year round, but particularly in heartier soups like our Super-vegie pumpkin soup, p36. They will keep for several weeks in

Soups are a fantastic way to work up to our five-plus serves of vegies a day – a large bowl can easily contain 2–3 serves.

a cool, dark and well-ventilated place out of plastic packaging.

Cans & packets

If you don't have time for their dried counterparts, canned beans, lentils and chickpeas are a convenient addition. Canned vegies and packets of dried legumes are also handy when their fresh varieties aren't in season.

TRY THIS When tomatoes are out of season, or just to save time, add canned tomatoes or bottled passata for richness.

Use low-fat coconut milk (also vegan) or cream to add creaminess to soups – it is delicious in Asian-style soups or even a classic pumpkin soup for a twist.

Stock up on dried pasta and dried or shelf-fresh Asian noodles – they keep well and can easily bulk up your soups.

Spices & aromatics!

Aromatic, tangy or exotic, the addition of fresh and/or dried spices will totally transform a simple soup into something mouth-watering, by adding a depth and complexity of flavour. By nature, spices are also low in calories and virtually fat free, which means they are also a fabulous way of upping taste without adding to your waistline.

TRY THIS Add fresh garlic, ginger, chilli or turmeric for natural antioxidants and anti-inflammatory compounds. Also add natural digestive aids, including crushed fennel seeds, coriander seeds, cinnamon and black pepper, to help relieve gas and bloating. If you have a lot of garlic, or you don't think you'll get around to using it all soon, you can always freeze it – just put unpeeled cloves in a sealable plastic bag. Ginger can be grated and frozen, as well.

With so many nourishing and filling combinations to try, soup is certain to become your new must-have, better-for-you meal. Soups also make the perfect thermos work lunch, too!

SOUPS FOR ALL SEASONS

Make soup your go-to healthy meal all year round, no matter what the weather.

Soups can be welcomed at the dining table at any time of the year, not only in cooler months.

Fresh peas, corn and tomatoes are at their best in warmer seasons, as are fennel and beans. Warm-climate vegies are delightful either whole, chopped, or pureed in lighter soups, including clear broths and even chilled soups. On the other hand, cool-climate vegetables, such as pumpkin, mushrooms, spinach and broccoli, beg to be made into thick and hearty soups to help keep you warmer on the inside when it's colder on the outside.

Keep an eye out for certain soups styles that work best with the type of meat and veg you are using. Think Asian-style and seafood soups for warmer days, and thicker root-vegie and grain soups for chunkier winter bowls. Take a look at our editor-in-chief's favourite seasonal soups in the table opposite for some inspiration.

Did you know that meats can be seasonal, too?. Lamb and salmon appear to be more prevalent when the weather is warmer. Meanwhile, you'll find more pork and beef around during the colder months, when the demand is greater for cuts like shoulder, leg and brisket. And fish, prawns and shellfish tend to prefer the shoulder seasons, when it's not too hot or cold.

Sure, you can buy most produce at the supermarket, even when they are out of season. However, if you make the most of seasonal vegetables, seafood and cuts of meat in your soups, they'll not only be at their nutritional and tasty best, they'll most likely be less expensive.

So where do you start? Why don't you head to the kitchen and check what produce you have at home right now, then turn to our index (p247) to see what delicious soups they can be made into? You'll be spoilt for choice!

SOUPS AT A GLANCE

Whether you need a soup to warm you up or to cool your mood,
choose from any one of these bowls of goodness.

E EASY   **FF** FAMILY-FRIENDLY   **GF** GLUTEN FREE   **LC** LOW-CAL   **Q** QUICK   **F** FREEZABLE

SUMMER

PORK & SWEETCORN WONTON
LC

CHICKEN & VEG CHILLI DRIZZLE
E **GF** **LC**

MEXICAN CHICKEN & CORN
E **FF** **GF**

ROASTED TOMATO & CAPSICUM
E **FF** **F**

HEALTHY CHICKEN NOODLE
E **FF** **GF** **LC**

AUTUMN

SUPER-VEGIE PUMPKIN
E **FF** **GF** **LC** **F**

GREEN CURRY & BROCCOLI,
E **GF** **LC**

RACY JAPANESE TOFU RAMEN
E **LC** **Q**

CREAMY BROCCOLI & 3-CHEESE
E **FF** **LC** **F**

SUPER BEETROOT & POTATO
E **FF** **GF** **LC** **F**

WINTER

SHREDDED CHICKEN NABE
E **FF** **LC**

CREAM OF ENGLISH SPINACH
E **F**

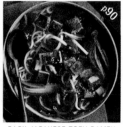

BUCKWHEAT & MUSHROOM
E **LC**

SPEEDY WINTER MINESTRONE
E **FF** **Q**

CAULIFLOWER & SANDWICH
E **FF** **Q** **F**

SPRING

ITALIAN FISH & PRAWN MEDLEY
E **LC**

SPRING VEGIE WITH FETA
E **FF** **LC** **Q**

JAPANESE SALMON NOODLE
E **Q**

SWEET POTATO & CHICKPEA
E **FF** **GF** **LC** **F**

VEG-LOADED CHICKEN
FF **LC** **F**

SOUPED UP!

Make your next soup stand out from the crockery crowd with these ideas for edible bowls and toppers.

COB LOAF

You can even eat this bowl! To make, cut top off a cob, scoop out centre and bake at 200°C/180°C fan forced for 20-30 minutes or until golden. Fill with a thick or pureed soup, such as a pumpkin or sweet potato soup.

COCONUT

We're all crazy for coconuts. The meat that lines the shell adds richness, so you don't need to add cream. To use, remove the top. Drain any liquid and reserve for a later use. Fill the coconut with a complementary soup, such as our Super greens & tofu crouton soup, p62.

TORTILLA

For a fabulous soup fiesta, try baked tortilla bowls. To make, preheat oven to 180°C/160°C fan forced. Press mini tortillas into pie tins or large muffin pans. Bake for 10 minutes or until crisp. Just before serving, fill with a thick or pureed soup, such as our 15-minute savoury pumpkin soup, p44 or the Black bean & chipotle soup, p206.

JAR

Small preserving jars are a clever non-spill way to transport individual servings of soup, for a picnic or lunch. To use, fill clean jars with hot soup and seal. The clear jar shows off delicious chunks of goodness in a soup such as our Chicken, chickpea & kale soup, p236.

CRISPY KALE LEAVES

Toss torn kale leaves in a little melted coconut oil. Season, then roast for 10 minutes or until crisp. Place on top of soup and sprinkle with dukkah.

BACON LATTICE

Interweave thin strips of bacon to create a lattice effect. Bake until crisp and golden. Place on top of soup and drizzle with a little maple syrup.

SWEET POTATO CHIPS

Use a mandoline to cut thin slices of sweet potato. Shallow-fry in vegetable oil until crisp. Drain on paper towel. Sprinkle with dried chilli flakes and sea salt.

GO TROPPO

Toss toasted coconut chips with shredded lime rind and thinly sliced long fresh green chilli.

CHEESY RAVIOLI

Dust fresh ravioli in plain flour, dip in whisked egg and coat in panko breadcrumbs. Deep-fry in vegetable oil until golden and crisp. Drain. Place on top of soup. Sprinkle with finely grated parmesan and baby basil leaves.

SPICED CHICKPEAS

Drain and pat dry canned chickpeas. Shallow-fry in extra virgin olive oil until crisp. Drain on paper towel. Toss with paprika, ground cumin and sea salt.

MEXICANA

Shallow-fry thinly sliced corn tortillas in vegetable oil until crisp. Drain. Top soup with tortillas, chopped avocado, chargrilled corn kernels and fresh coriander leaves.

PARMESAN TUILES

Mix 140g (2 cups) finely grated parmesan with 2 tsp plain flour. Sprinkle clusters over a baking tray lined with baking paper. Bake for 10 minutes or until golden and melted. Cool. Place on top of soup. Sprinkle with finely chopped fresh chives.

HAM & CHEESE CROUTONS

Sandwich bread with shaved leg ham and grated cheddar. Cut off crusts. Pan-fry in butter and olive oil until golden. Cut into triangles.

JAPANESE, PLEASE

Shallow-fry julienned ginger in peanut oil until crisp. Drain. Toss with thinly sliced nori sheets, podded edamame and toasted sesame seeds.

QUICKER TO LADLE

DELICIOUS SOUPS ON THE TABLE IN UNDER AN HOUR.
ALL THE FLAVOUR; A FRACTION OF THE LABOUR!

TOMATO, FENNEL & MEATBALL

Turn soup from a starter into a hearty main with mouth-watering meatballs that will have the family asking for "more, please"!

SERVES 4 **PREP** 10 mins **COOK** 40 mins

2 fennel bulbs, trimmed, fronds reserved

1 tbs extra virgin olive oil

1 brown onion, finely chopped

2 garlic cloves, crushed

1L (4 cups) gluten-free chicken stock

2 x 400g cans chopped tomatoes

1 tsp caster sugar

400g cooked gluten-free bought or pre-made pork and veal meatballs

2 tbs chopped fresh continental parsley leaves

1 Thinly slice the fennel bulbs. Heat the oil in a large saucepan over medium heat. Add the onion. Cook, stirring, for 5 minutes or until onion has softened. Add the garlic and fennel. Cook, stirring often, for 10 minutes or until fennel has softened.

2 Stir in the stock, tomato and sugar. Season. Cover and bring to the boil. Reduce the heat to medium-low and simmer for 15 minutes.

3 Add the meatballs. Simmer for 10 minutes or until meatballs are heated through. Season. Serve soup sprinkled with parsley and reserved fennel fronds.

COOK'S TIP

For a change of flavour, you can replace the pork and veal with beef, lamb or chicken meatballs.

NUTRITION (PER SERVE)

CALS	FAT	SAT FAT	PROTEIN	CARBS
355	15g	3.9g	28.6g	24.4g

● EASY ● FAMILY-FRIENDLY ● GLUTEN FREE ● LOW CAL ○ QUICK ● FREEZABLE

PRAWN & SALMON CHOWDER

You'll be surprised at the wonderful richness of this easy seafood chowder, even though it's cooked for such a brief time.

SERVES 4 **PREP** 10 mins **COOK** 10 mins

400g pkt microwave baby potatoes with butter and herbs
60ml (¼ cup) olive oil
100g bought diced bacon
1 leek, trimmed, sliced
2 garlic cloves, crushed
2 tbs plain flour
500ml (2 cups) milk or almond milk
310ml (1¼ cups) chicken stock
250g skinless salmon fillet, cut into 2cm pieces
16 peeled green prawns, tails intact
420g can corn kernels, drained
2 fresh continental parsley sprigs, leaves coarsely chopped

1 Heat a large deep frying pan over high heat. Cook the potatoes in the microwave following packet directions.

2 Meanwhile, heat the oil in a large, deep frying pan over high heat. Add the bacon, leek and garlic. Cook, stirring, for 2-3 minutes or until leek is softened. Add the flour and cook, stirring, for 30 seconds or until well combined. Remove pan from the heat.

3 Gradually add the milk and stock to the leek mixture, stirring until smooth and well combined. Place pan over medium-high heat and cook, stirring, until the mixture comes to a gentle simmer. Add the salmon, prawns and corn. Cook, stirring occasionally, for 2-3 minutes or until the salmon and prawns are cooked through.

4 Thickly slice the potatoes and divide among serving bowls. Ladle in the seafood chowder. Scatter with parsley, to serve.

COOK'S TIP

If you prefer, replace the salmon with a firm white fish fillet, such as ling or barramundi.

NUTRITION (PER SERVE)

CALS	FAT	SAT FAT	PROTEIN	CARBS
622	36g	8.4g	39.1g	33.8g

● EASY ● FAMILY-FRIENDLY ○ GLUTEN FREE ○ LOW CAL ● QUICK ○ FREEZABLE

★★★★★ *Sooo easy and delicious.*
A great midweek dish for our family **SHAWNTHEPRAWN**

10 minutes prep

FRENCH-STYLE SEAFOOD

Ready in just 15 minutes, this flavourful soup utilises a zero-prep marinara mix and begs you to sop up every last drop with the crusty bread.

SERVES 4 **PREP** 5 mins **COOK** 10 mins

- 2 tbs olive oil
- 1 small fennel bulb, trimmed, fronds reserved
- 1 small onion, halved, thinly sliced
- 1 tbs gluten-free chicken stock powder
- 400g btl passata
- 750ml (3 cups) boiling water
- 500g seafood marinara mix
- 100g (1 cup) frozen sliced green beans
- 85g (⅓ cup) aïoli
- 4 slices crusty bread, toasted

1. Heat the oil in a large saucepan over medium-high heat. Halve the fennel bulb and thinly slice. Add the fennel and onion to the pan. Cook, stirring occasionally, for 4 minutes or until softened.

2. Add the stock powder, passata and boiling water. Cover and bring to a simmer. Add the marinara mix and beans. Cover and return to a simmer. Cook for 2 minutes or until the seafood is opaque and just cooked through. Season.

3. Ladle the soup among serving bowls. Dollop with the aïoli and sprinkle with the reserved fennel fronds. Serve with the toast.

NUTRITION (PER SERVE)

CALS	FAT	SAT FAT	PROTEIN	CARBS
562	35.5g	5.9g	32.6g	26.7g

COOK'S TIP

Marinara mix saves on prep time. If frozen, when adding in step 2, simmer for a few minutes before adding the beans. You can use the same weight of chopped boneless fish fillet or raw prawns, if you prefer.

★★★★★ *Quick and super easy to make. I can be home from work after 5pm and have a delicious meal on the table by 6pm.* **FEEZY**

● EASY ○ FAMILY-FRIENDLY ○ GLUTEN FREE ○ LOW CAL ● QUICK ○ FREEZABLE

CLASSIC FRENCH
ONION

This rich aromatic soup will bring a little 70s retro to your dining table and a disco to your tastebuds. The cheesy toast is a highlight.

SERVES 4 **PREP** 10 mins **COOK** 45 mins

1 tbs olive oil
50g butter, chopped
750g brown onions, halved, thinly sliced
3 tsp brown sugar
2 tbs plain flour
80ml (⅓ cup) dry apera (sherry)
1L (4 cups) beef stock
1 dried bay leaf
3 sprigs fresh thyme
30cm baguette, cut into 1.5cm-thick slices
80g (1 cup) grated gruyère

1 Heat the oil and butter in a large saucepan over medium heat. Add the onion and reduce the heat to low. Cook, stirring, for 10 minutes or until the onion has softened. Increase the heat to medium. Add the sugar and cook, stirring, for 8 minutes or until caramelised.

2 Add the flour. Cook, stirring, for 1 minute. Add the apera. Cook, stirring, for 1 minute or until mixture bubbles and thickens. Gradually stir in the stock. Add 500ml (2 cups) water, the bay leaf and thyme. Season. Bring to the boil. Reduce the heat to low. Simmer for 20 minutes.

3 Meanwhile, preheat an oven grill. Spray both sides of bread with oil. Place on a baking tray. Bake for 2 minutes or until tops are golden. Turn over. Bake for 1 minute or until just starting to brown. Sprinkle with cheese. Bake for 2 minutes or until cheese is melted.

4 Discard bay leaf and thyme from soup. Ladle soup among serving bowls. Top with toast. Season. Serve.

COOK'S TIP

This soup can be frozen. Cool completely then place in an airtight container. Freeze for up to 2 months. Don't forget to label and date!

NUTRITION (PER SERVE)

CALS	FAT	SAT FAT	PROTEIN	CARBS
547	25.8g	13g	22.4g	50g

★★★★★ *Really easy and really tasty.* **RILEY**

● EASY   ● FAMILY-FRIENDLY   ○ GLUTEN FREE   ○ LOW CAL   ○ QUICK   ● FREEZABLE

ZUCCHINI & BORLOTTI MINESTRONE

For a warming soup without the extra calories, we added nutritious vegies, such as zucchini and borlotti beans, to your typical minestrone.

SERVES 4 **PREP** 20 mins **COOK** 25 mins

60ml (¼ cup) extra virgin olive oil, plus extra, to drizzle

3 bacon rashers, sliced

2 large desiree potatoes, scrubbed, cut into 1cm pieces

1 leek, thinly sliced

1 red onion, finely chopped

4 garlic cloves, finely chopped

1 tbs tomato paste

3 zucchini, thinly sliced

750ml (3 cups) gluten-free chicken stock

400g can borlotti beans, rinsed, drained

400g can chickpeas, rinsed, drained

1-2 lemons, juiced

Shaved parmesan and fresh celery or continental parsley leaves, to serve

1 Heat half the oil in a large saucepan over medium heat. Add the bacon, potato, leek, onion and garlic. Cook, stirring occasionally, for 10 minutes or until leek and onion are softened and golden. Stir in the tomato paste.

2 Add the zucchini and remaining oil. Cook for 5 minutes or until zucchini is light golden.

3 Pour in the stock and cook for 5 minutes or until the potato is tender. Add the borlotti beans and chickpeas. Stir in the lemon juice, to taste. Cook for 1-2 minutes or until warmed through. Season.

4 Ladle the soup among serving bowls. Drizzle over the extra oil and top with the parmesan and celery or parsley leaves, to serve.

COOK'S TIP

If you can, use a collagen-rich homemade chicken bone broth to make this extra nourishing.

NUTRITION (PER SERVE)

CALS	FAT	SAT FAT	PROTEIN	CARBS
493	27.2g	6.3g	22.5g	34.6g

★★★★★ *Absolutely loved the flavour of it. It also provides more than four standard servings.* **TAHLIASEATS**

● EASY ● FAMILY-FRIENDLY ● GLUTEN FREE ○ LOW CAL ○ QUICK ● FREEZABLE

20
minutes
prep

HEARTY FRENCH CHICKEN

Try this super-easy classic French soup that is high in fibre and will keep the family full. The flavours get richer over time, making it great for leftovers.

SERVES 4 **PREP** 10 mins **COOK** 45 mins

1 tbs extra virgin olive oil
4 chicken thigh fillets, trimmed
1 brown onion, halved, sliced
3 carrots, halved, thickly sliced diagonally
2 celery stalks, thickly sliced diagonally
3 garlic cloves, thinly sliced
1 dried bay leaf
3 sprigs fresh thyme
80ml (⅓ cup) dry white wine
1L (4 cups) chicken stock
500g potato, peeled, cut into pieces
Finely chopped and whole fresh continental parsley leaves, and toasted sliced baguette, to serve

1 Heat the oil in a large saucepan over high heat. Season chicken and add to the pan. Cook for 4 minutes on each side or until browned. Transfer to a plate.

2 Add the onion, carrot, celery, garlic, bay leaf and thyme to the pan. Reduce heat to medium. Cook, stirring occasionally, for 6 minutes or until vegies are well browned. Add the wine. Cook, scraping base of pan, for 1 minute. Return the chicken to the pan and stir in the stock and potato. Bring to the boil. Simmer, covered, for 25 minutes or until vegies are tender and chicken is cooked.

3 Use tongs to transfer chicken to a board. Using 2 forks, shred chicken. Remove and discard bay leaf and thyme.

4 Return chicken to the pan and simmer for 2 minutes. Ladle soup among serving bowls. Sprinkle with parsley. Season with pepper. Serve with the toast.

COOK'S TIP

For a more substantial soup, bulk it up with a few sliced Swiss brown mushrooms and a handful of baby spinach leaves. Add with the chicken in step 4.

NUTRITION (PER SERVE)

CALS	FAT	SAT FAT	PROTEIN	CARBS
567	15.7g	3.8g	41g	56.6g

● EASY ● FAMILY-FRIENDLY ○ GLUTEN FREE ○ LOW CAL ○ QUICK ○ FREEZABLE

10
minutes
prep

SUPER-VEGIE
PUMPKIN

This pumpkin soup is packed with so many vegies, it makes the perfect dish to help your family reach their five-a-day minimum. The kids will love it, too!

SERVES 8 **PREP** 20 mins **COOK** 40 mins

2kg butternut pumpkin, peeled, deseeded, chopped
2 large brown onions, chopped
4 carrots, chopped
4 middle bacon rashers, trimmed, chopped, plus extra 2 rashers, trimmed, finely chopped
4 sebago potatoes, peeled, chopped
2 parsnips, peeled, chopped
½ tsp ground nutmeg
2L (8 cups) gluten-free chicken stock
2 tsp olive oil
2 tbs pure cream
Chopped fresh chives, to serve

1 Place the pumpkin, onion, carrot, bacon, potato, parsnip, nutmeg and stock in a large saucepan over high heat. Cover and bring to the boil. Reduce the heat to medium. Simmer for 35 minutes or until vegetables are tender. Remove from the heat. Stand for 5 minutes.

2 Meanwhile, heat the oil in a frying pan over medium-high heat. Cook the extra bacon for 4-5 minutes or until golden and crisp. Transfer to a plate lined with paper towel.

3 Using a stick blender, blend soup in pan until smooth. Season well. Serve soup drizzled with cream and sprinkled with fried bacon and chives.

COOK'S TIP

Adjust the thickness of this soup to your liking using extra stock, water or milk.

NUTRITION (PER SERVE)

CALS	FAT	SAT FAT	PROTEIN	CARBS
297	6.1g	2.4g	13.8g	41g

★★★★★ *Wow! It's packed with flavour – rich but light at the same time! This recipe is going to replace my old go-to.* **CATALYST**

● EASY ● FAMILY-FRIENDLY ● GLUTEN FREE ● LOW CAL ○ QUICK ● FREEZABLE

20 *minutes prep*

KETO CAULIFLOWER &
BACON

Thick and creamy, this warming and fulfilling soup will be on high rotation in your household. Pop it into a school or work thermos for lunch on the go.

SERVES 4 **PREP** 10 mins **COOK** 30 mins

25g butter
2 green shallots, thinly sliced, white and green sections separated
800g cauliflower, cut into florets
750ml (3 cups) gluten-free chicken stock
250ml (1 cup) thickened cream, plus extra, to drizzle
180g bacon, thinly sliced
Extra virgin olive oil, to drizzle
25g (⅓ cup) shaved parmesan

1 Heat the butter in a large saucepan over medium heat until foamy. Add white section of the shallot and cook, stirring, for 1 minute or until softened.

2 Add the cauliflower. Stir to coat. Pour in the stock and bring to a simmer. Reduce heat to low. Simmer, partially covered, for 20 minutes or until cauliflower is tender. Stir in the cream. Set aside to cool slightly.

3 Meanwhile, cook the bacon in a frying pan over medium-high heat, stirring occasionally, for 5 minutes or until crisp. Remove from the heat.

4 Use a stick blender to blend the soup in the pan until smooth. Bring the soup to a simmer over high heat. Season with salt.

5 Ladle soup among serving bowls. Drizzle over the extra cream and olive oil. Season. Serve sprinkled with bacon, parmesan and green section of shallot.

COOK'S TIP

Serve this soup with garlic bread for dipping and sopping up any soup still clinging to the bowl.

NUTRITION (PER SERVE)

CALS	FAT	SAT FAT	PROTEIN	CARBS
550	51.2g	27.2g	14.5g	8.9g

● EASY ● FAMILY-FRIENDLY ● GLUTEN FREE ○ LOW CAL ○ QUICK ● FREEZABLE

SHREDDED CHICKEN NABE

Quick and easy, this Japanese hot-pot-style soup is made with low-cal lean chicken breast. The wombok adds nutrients, texture and subtle sweetness.

SERVES 4 **PREP** 10 mins **COOK** 20 mins

1 tbs extra virgin olive oil
700g chicken breast fillets
1L (4 cups) chicken stock
2 carrots, peeled, halved
    lengthways, sliced diagonally
½ wombok (Chinese cabbage),
    trimmed, thinly shredded
75g (¼ cup) white miso paste
2 tbs cooking sake (see tip)
2 tbs light soy sauce
1 tbs caster sugar
2 green shallots, trimmed, chopped

1 Heat the oil in a large deep frying pan over medium heat. Add the chicken and cook for 7 minutes on each side or until just cooked through. Transfer to a plate. Cool slightly. Use fingers to shred the chicken.

2 Add the stock and carrot to the pan. Bring to the boil and simmer for 5 minutes. Add the cabbage and simmer for 4 minutes. Combine the miso, cooking sake, soy sauce and sugar in a bowl. Add a little stock liquid and stir until miso dissolves. Stir into the pan.

3 Ladle soup among bowls. Top with the chicken. Sprinkle with the shallot, to serve.

NUTRITION (PER SERVE)

CALS	FAT	SAT FAT	PROTEIN	CARBS
338	10g	2g	45g	13g

COOK'S TIP

The Japanese use sake for cooking, the same way that Western countries use wine. You can substitute sake for mirin or dry vermouth, but using sake will achieve the best results.

★★★★★

Quick and easy, liked it. **DRPRETTY**

● EASY ● FAMILY-FRIENDLY ○ GLUTEN FREE ● LOW CAL ○ QUICK ○ FREEZABLE

HEARTY CHORIZO & POTATO

This main-meal soup is a cinch to make. We recommend you make double batch – it tastes even better the next day!

SERVES 4 **PREP** 15 mins **COOK** 35 mins

1 tsp extra virgin olive oil
1 chorizo, thinly sliced
1 red onion, finely chopped
1 tsp mild paprika
1 tbs tomato paste
500g desiree potatoes, peeled, coarsely chopped
1 red capsicum, chopped
125g can corn kernels, drained
1 tomato, chopped
1L (4 cups) salt-reduced chicken stock
⅓ cup chopped fresh continental parsley leaves, plus extra leaves, to serve
¼ tsp dried chilli flakes
Sliced crusty bread, to serve

1 Heat the oil in a large saucepan over medium-high heat. Add the chorizo. Cook, stirring, for 3 minutes or until browned. Add the onion. Cook, stirring, for 5 minutes or until the onion is softened. Add the paprika and tomato paste. Cook, stirring, for 1 minute or until well combined.

2 Add the potato, capsicum, corn, tomato and stock. Bring to the boil. Reduce heat to low. Simmer, covered, for 15-20 minutes or until the potato is tender. Stir in the parsley. Season.

3 Ladle the soup among serving bowls. Sprinkle with chilli and extra parsley. Serve with crusty bread.

COOK'S TIP

Add shredded cooked chicken to make this soup even more hearty.

NUTRITION (PER SERVE)

CALS	FAT	SAT FAT	PROTEIN	CARBS
424	14.4g	4g	17.2g	52.4g

★★★★★

Simple hearty soup to whip up quickly when you need comfort food. Very versatile depending on what you have in the fridge. **ELWOOD13**

● EASY ● FAMILY-FRIENDLY ○ GLUTEN FREE ● LOW CAL ○ QUICK ● FREEZABLE

15-MIN SAVOURY PUMPKIN

Pre-chopped veg saves on prep time and bacon adds plenty of flavour to this pumpkin soup that's ready before the kids even get to the dining table.

SERVES 4 **PREP** 5 mins **COOK** 10 mins

2 x 500g pkts frozen pumpkin cubes
1L (4 cups) gluten-free chicken stock
80g (½ cup) bought diced bacon
70g (½ cup) chopped frozen onion
3 tsp ground cumin
80g feta
Roasted lightly salted chickpeas,
    to serve
Fresh lemon thyme and dried chilli
    flakes (optional), to serve

1 Place the pumpkin and stock in a large saucepan over high heat. Cover and bring to the boil. Cook for 4 minutes or until the pumpkin is tender. Remove from the heat.

2 Meanwhile, cook the bacon in a frying pan over medium-high heat for 3 minutes or until starting to crisp. Transfer to a plate lined with paper towel to drain. Add the onion to the pan and cook, stirring, for 2 minutes or until softened. Add cumin. Cook for 30 seconds or until aromatic.

3 Add the onion mixture to the pumpkin and stock. Use a stick blender to blend soup in the pan until smooth. Ladle soup among serving bowls. Crumble the feta on top. Sprinkle with the bacon, chickpeas, thyme and chilli, if using. Season with black pepper, to serve.

COOK'S TIP

Omit the bacon for a vegetarian dish, or try sprinkling with dried shallots for an added savoury flavour.

NUTRITION (PER SERVE)

CALS	FAT	SAT FAT	PROTEIN	CARBS
291	12g	5.2g	15.7g	40g

● EASY ● FAMILY-FRIENDLY ● GLUTEN FREE ● LOW CAL ● QUICK ● FREEZABLE

★★★★★ *The bacon, feta and chickpeas really lift this classic soup. We can't get enough!* **SHAWNSALAD**

CREAMY CHICKEN & CORN

There is no need for Chinese takeaway when this family-friendly soup is so quick and easy to make. You can bet it's MSG-free, too!

SERVES 4 **PREP** 10 mins **COOK** 30 mins

1 tbs rice bran oil
250g chicken breast fillet, chopped
1L (4 cups) gluten-free chicken stock
420g can creamed corn
2 x 125g cans corn kernels, drained
2 tbs gluten-free cornflour
60ml (¼ cup) pouring cream
1 egg, lightly whisked
2 green shallots, thinly sliced,
    plus extra, to serve

1 Heat the oil in a large saucepan over medium-high heat. Add the chicken. Cook, stirring, for 3-5 minutes or until browned all over.

2 Add stock, creamed corn, corn kernels and 250ml (1 cup) water to the pan. Bring to the boil. Reduce heat to low and simmer, stirring occasionally, for 10 minutes.

3 Meanwhile, combine the cornflour in a jug with 2 tbs water until smooth. Increase pan heat to medium-high. Gradually stir cornflour mixture into the soup. Add the cream and bring to the boil. Reduce heat to low. Simmer, stirring occasionally, for 5 minutes or until soup thickens.

4 Remove pan from the heat. Add egg in a slow, steady stream, stirring constantly, to form ribbons throughout the soup. Stir in the shallot. Season well with pepper. Serve soup topped with extra shallot.

COOK'S TIP

Make your prep time even quicker by adding barbecued chicken in place of cooked breast fillet. Simply shred the meat and add before simmering in step 3.

NUTRITION (PER SERVE)

CALS	FAT	SAT FAT	PROTEIN	CARBS
323	13.8g	5.6g	19.6g	28.1g

● EASY ● FAMILY-FRIENDLY ● GLUTEN FREE ● LOW CAL ○ QUICK ○ FREEZABLE

10 minutes prep

★★★★★

I have made this soup a couple of times now and just had to say thank you so much for such an amazingly easy and yummy soup! **SHELL**

HEARTY RICE & GREENS

This good-for-you soup will keep you warm and full. With three serves of vegies per bowl, you can easily get a wholesome boost of greens.

SERVES 4 **PREP** 10 mins **COOK** 20 mins

1½ tbs extra virgin olive oil
2 middle bacon rashers, trimmed, chopped (see tip)
500g pkt frozen peas
1 brown onion, finely chopped
2 garlic cloves, finely chopped
1.5L (6 cups) gluten-free chicken stock
150g (¾ cup) jasmine rice
250g pkt frozen chopped spinach, thawed
100g smooth feta, crumbled
Fresh mint leaves, to serve

1 Heat 2 tsp oil in a large saucepan over medium-high heat. Add bacon. Cook, stirring, for 2-3 minutes or until golden and crisp. Transfer to a plate lined with paper towel to drain. Use paper towel to wipe fat from pan.

2 Meanwhile, place peas in a heatproof bowl. Cover with boiling water. Stand for 2 minutes. Drain. Transfer half the peas to a food processor. Process until almost smooth.

3 Heat remaining oil in the pan over medium heat. Add onion and garlic. Cook, stirring, for 3 minutes. Add stock. Increase heat to high and bring to the boil. Stir in rice and processed peas. Cook for 10 minutes or until rice is tender. Add spinach and remaining peas. Bring to the boil. Serve soup topped with bacon, feta and mint.

COOK'S TIP

Worried about saturated fat? Instead of middle rashers, use short cut bacon or reduced-fat ham.

NUTRITION (PER SERVE)

CALS	FAT	SAT FAT	PROTEIN	CARBS
421	4.9g	23.1g	46.9g	9.5g

★★★★★

This soup not only looks good, but tastes good, too. Will make again for sure. **CMONSTER**

● EASY ● FAMILY-FRIENDLY ● GLUTEN FREE ● LOW CAL ● QUICK ○ FREEZABLE

GREEN TEA &
DUMPLING

A super-quick nourishing soup that doesn't have to bubble away for hours in order to taste amazing. Chopsticks are optional!

SERVES 4 **PREP** 5 mins **COOK** 15 mins

1L (4 cups) vegetable
  or chicken stock
1 tbs sesame seeds
2 green shallots
100g fresh shiitake mushrooms
1 bunch broccolini
4 green tea teabags, tags removed
240g pkt frozen prawn & chive
  wontons
80g (½ cup) podded frozen edamame
2 tsp soy sauce

1 Place the stock in a large deep frying pan over high heat and bring to the boil.

2 Meanwhile, place the sesame seeds in a small frying pan over medium-low heat. Cook, stirring occasionally, for 2 minutes or until toasted. Thinly slice the shallots. Thickly slice any large mushrooms. Cut the broccolini in half lengthways.

3 Add the teabags, wontons, edamame and broccolini to the stock with the 2 soup sachets from the wonton packet. Add 500ml (2 cups) water and return to the boil. Simmer for 5 minutes or until wontons are cooked through.

4 Remove and discard the teabags. Stir in the soy sauce. Ladle soup among serving bowls and sprinkle with sesame seeds and shallot, to serve.

COOK'S TIP

To make this soup vegetarian, use vegie wontons and a plant-based stock.

NUTRITION (PER SERVE)

CALS	FAT	SAT FAT	PROTEIN	CARBS
158	5.8g	1g	9.5g	14.7g

● EASY   ○ FAMILY-FRIENDLY   ○ GLUTEN FREE   ● LOW CAL   ● QUICK   ○ FREEZABLE

★★★★★ *What a yummy soup! I change it up by using different flavoured wontons each time I make it.* **HUSBO**

ITALIAN FISH & PRAWN MEDLEY

This soup's got a whole lotta flavour and is blessedly low in fat and calories. The cannellini beans add fibre to fully satisfy.

SERVES 4 **PREP** 20 mins **COOK** 30 mins

8 thin slices sourdough baguette
1 garlic clove, halved, plus
    extra 2 garlic cloves, crushed
1 brown onion, finely chopped
2 celery sticks, finely chopped
1 baby fennel bulb, trimmed,
    finely chopped
¼ tsp dried chilli flakes
400g can diced tomatoes
1 dried bay leaf
400g can cannellini beans, rinsed,
    drained
400g firm white fish fillets, cut into
    2cm pieces
250g peeled medium green prawns
1 zucchini, halved, thinly sliced
Chopped fresh continental parsley,
    to serve

1 Preheat oven to 200°C/180°C fan forced. Rub each side of bread with the cut side of the garlic clove half. Place on a baking tray and spray with olive oil. Bake, turning halfway, for 10-12 minutes or until golden and crisp.

2 Meanwhile, heat a saucepan over medium heat. Spray with oil. Add the onion, celery and fennel. Cook, stirring, for 6-7 minutes or until vegies are softened. Add the garlic and chilli flakes. Cook for 1 minute or until aromatic.

3 Stir 750ml (3 cups) water, the tomato and bay leaf into the onion mixture. Bring to the boil. Reduce heat to low and simmer for 10 minutes. Add beans, fish, prawns and zucchini. Simmer for 5 minutes or until the seafood is just cooked and the zucchini is tender. Ladle soup among serving bowls. Season with pepper. Sprinkle with parsley. Serve with garlic toast.

COOK'S TIP

For a subtle nutty flavour, replace the cannellini beans with cooked pearl barley. Add 1 cup cooked pearl barley after stirring in the tomato and water in step 3.

NUTRITION (PER SERVE)

CALS	FAT	SAT FAT	PROTEIN	CARBS
370	15g	0.5g	47g	34g

● EASY   ○ FAMILY-FRIENDLY   ○ GLUTEN FREE   ● LOW CAL   ○ QUICK   ○ FREEZABLE

★★★★★ *Very filling and the seafood is nicely tender.* **CMON**

ITALIAN SAUSAGE &
LENTIL

An easy sausage soup that is quick to make and very filling. Loaded with veg, the nutritious bowl boasts a good measure of protein and fibre.

SERVES 4 **PREP** 10 mins **COOK** 25 mins

2 tbs extra virgin olive oil

400g pork and fennel sausages,
  casings removed

1 brown onion, finely chopped

1 carrot, peeled, finely chopped

1 baby fennel bulb, finely chopped

1 stick celery, finely chopped

3 garlic cloves, crushed

1 tbs tomato paste

1L (4 cups) beef stock

400g can brown lentils,
  rinsed, drained

1 small bunch Tuscan kale,
  leaves thinly sliced

Parmesan toast, to serve (optional)

1 Heat 2 tsp oil in a large saucepan over medium heat. Add the sausage meat and cook, breaking up meat with a wooden spoon, for 5 minutes or until browned. Use a slotted spoon to transfer meat to a bowl.

2 Heat the remaining oil in the pan over medium heat. Add the onion, carrot, fennel, celery and garlic. Cook, stirring occasionally, for 5 minutes or until vegies are softened. Stir in the tomato paste.

3 Stir the stock and 250ml (1 cup) water into the pan. Cover and bring to a simmer. Simmer for 4 minutes. Add the lentils and sausage meat. Simmer, covered, for 2 minutes or until warmed through. Add the kale and simmer, covered, for 2 minutes or until just wilted. Serve with parmesan toast, if desired.

COOK'S TIP

Don't have enough time to chop the vegies? Throw them all into a food processor and process until just finely chopped.

NUTRITION (PER SERVE)

CALS	FAT	SAT FAT	PROTEIN	CARBS
514	30g	10g	29g	28g

● EASY   ● FAMILY-FRIENDLY   ○ GLUTEN FREE   ○ LOW CAL   ○ QUICK   ● FREEZABLE

10 minutes prep

★★★★★

My 4-year-old requests this soup, as does my 80-year-old neighbour. Total crowd-pleaser, easy to make and delicious. **KCSUNSHINE**

QUINOA, FETA &
BROCCOLI

This weeknight wonder is super easy and packed with healthy goodness – plus, it's low cal. Winner, winner broccoli dinner!

SERVES 4 **PREP** 10 mins **COOK** 30 mins

70g (⅓ cup) tri-coloured quinoa
1 tbs extra virgin olive oil,
    plus extra, to serve
1 brown onion, finely chopped
2 garlic cloves, crushed
2 (about 300g) potatoes,
    peeled, chopped
1 large head (about 480g) broccoli,
    stems and florets separated
1L (4 cups) gluten-free chicken stock
100g baby spinach leaves
½ cup fresh mint leaves
1 small lemon, rind finely
    grated, juiced
80g reduced-fat smooth
    feta, crumbled
Baby herbs, to serve (optional)

1 Place the quinoa and 150ml water in a saucepan over high heat. Bring to the boil. Reduce heat to low. Cook, covered, stirring occasionally, for 10-12 minutes or until just tender. Drain and refresh under cold running water.

2 Meanwhile, heat the oil in a saucepan over medium heat. Add the onion and garlic. Cook, stirring, for 5 minutes or until softened. Stir in the potato and broccoli stems. Add the stock and 100ml water. Bring to the boil over high heat. Reduce heat to medium and simmer for 10 minutes or until potato is almost soft.

3 Add broccoli florets to the soup. Simmer for 6 minutes or until just tender. Add the spinach and mint. Simmer for 1 minute or until wilted. Use a stick blender to process soup in the pan until smooth. Stir in lemon juice. Season.

4 Ladle soup among serving bowls. Top with the quinoa, lemon rind, feta and baby herbs, if using. Drizzle with extra oil, to serve.

COOK'S TIP

Want even more greens? Add a handful of chopped kale and/or chopped parsley with the mint in step 3.

NUTRITION (PER SERVE)

CALS	FAT	SAT FAT	PROTEIN	CARBS
278	12g	3g	16g	22g

● EASY   ○ FAMILY-FRIENDLY   ● GLUTEN FREE   ● LOW CAL   ○ QUICK   ● FREEZABLE

*A really delicious, healthy soup.
I've made this many times.* **KATIEMARIE**

CAULIFLOWER & HAM SANDWICH

Mini ham and cheese sandwiches are served on top of this creamy cauliflower soup for a deliciously hearty soup the whole family will adore.

SERVES 4 **PREP** 10 mins **COOK** 15 mins

25g butter
2 tsp olive oil, plus extra, to serve
1 leek, thinly sliced
850g cauliflower, chopped
250g sebago potatoes, peeled,
    coarsely chopped
1.25L (5 cups) chicken stock
120g blue cheese, crumbled
8 slices white bread
20g smoked ham
125ml (½ cup) thickened cream
Baby radish leaves,
    to serve (optional)

1 Heat the butter and oil in a large saucepan over medium-high heat. Add the leek and cook, stirring, for 3 minutes or until softened. Add the cauliflower, potato and stock. Bring to the boil and simmer for 12 minutes or until potato is tender. Remove from the heat.

2 Meanwhile, crumble blue cheese over 4 slices white bread. Top with ham. Top each with another slice of bread. Spray a large non-stick frying pan with oil. Fry sandwiches for 2 minutes on each side or until golden. Cut each sandwich into triangles.

3 Use a stick blender to blend soup in the pan until smooth. Stir in the cream. Ladle soup among serving bowls. Top with the sandwich triangles. Drizzle with extra oil. Top with baby leaves, if using, and serve.

COOK'S TIP

Omit the ham and use a plant-based chicken stock to make this soup a vegetarian meal.

NUTRITION (PER SERVE)

CALS	FAT	SAT FAT	PROTEIN	CARBS
552	25.5g	13.5g	19.8g	64.4g

★★★★★ *A fun soup that we all love to get stuck into.* **MURRAY50**

● EASY ● FAMILY-FRIENDLY ○ GLUTEN FREE ○ LOW CAL ● QUICK ● FREEZABLE

15-MIN CHICKEN &
TORTELLINI

This quick and easy 4-step soup uses packet tortellini so you don't have to make it from scratch. It's also low-cal and packed with veg.

SERVES 4 **PREP** 5 mins **COOK** 10 mins

1.5L (6 cups) chicken stock
300g chicken tenderloins, sliced
325g pkt fresh spinach and
  ricotta tortellini
250g frozen broccoli florets
150g (1 cup) frozen peas
Bought tomato pesto and finely
  grated parmesan, to serve

1 Pour the stock into a large saucepan. Cover and bring to the boil over high heat.

2 Add the chicken and tortellini to the stock. Cover and return to the boil. Partially cover. Cook for 2 minutes.

3 Add the broccoli and peas to the pan. Cook for 2 minutes or until heated through.

4 Ladle soup among serving bowls. Top with a dollop of pesto. Sprinkle with parmesan, to serve.

COOK'S TIP

You can use different flavoured tortellini, or even wontons in this soup, if preferred.

NUTRITION (PER SERVE)

CALS	FAT	SAT FAT	PROTEIN	CARBS
335	8.2g	3.1g	30.9g	29.8g

★★★★★

Great for a quick meal. **MARY JULIA**

● EASY ○ FAMILY-FRIENDLY ○ GLUTEN FREE ● LOW CAL ● QUICK ○ FREEZABLE

SUPER GREENS & TOFU CROUTON

Broccoli, coriander and spinach combine for a quick soup with sensational flavour. The chilli and lemongrass tofu topper is out of this world!

SERVES 4 **PREP** 15 mins **COOK** 15 mins

2 tbs coconut oil

1 brown onion, coarsely chopped

½ bunch fresh coriander, roots finely chopped, leaves picked, plus extra leaves, to serve

3cm-piece fresh ginger, peeled, finely chopped

3 garlic cloves, 2 thinly sliced, 1 crushed

500g fresh broccoli, stems sliced, head cut into florets

1L (4 cups) vegetable stock

1 lemongrass stem, white part only, finely chopped

1 fresh long red chilli, deseeded, finely chopped

15g palm sugar, finely chopped

250g firm tofu, coarsely chopped

2 tsp fish sauce, or to taste

120g baby spinach, plus extra, to serve

1 lime, rind finely grated, juiced

Light coconut milk, to drizzle (optional)

1 Heat 1 tbs oil in a large saucepan over medium heat. Add the onion, coriander root, ginger, sliced garlic and broccoli stems. Cook, stirring, for 4 minutes or until softened. Add the stock. Bring to the boil.

2 Add the broccoli florets to the pan. Simmer, stirring occasionally, for 6 minutes or until just tender.

3 Meanwhile, heat the remaining oil in a non-stick frying pan over medium heat. Add the lemongrass, chilli and palm sugar. Cook, stirring, for 30 seconds or until aromatic. Add tofu. Cook, stirring, for 4 minutes. Add crushed garlic and fish sauce. Cook, stirring, for 1 minute or until tofu is golden.

4 Stir the spinach and coriander leaves into the pan. Remove from the heat. Stir in the lime rind and juice. Use a stick blender to blend soup in the pan until smooth.

5 Ladle soup among serving bowls. Drizzle with coconut milk, if using. Top with the tofu, plus the extra spinach and coriander leaves. Serve.

COOK'S TIP

Prepare this soup up to 1 day in advance, omitting the lime juice until it is reheated. Cook the tofu just before serving.

NUTRITION (PER SERVE)

CALS	FAT	SAT FAT	PROTEIN	CARBS
280	15g	9g	17g	13g

○ EASY   ● FAMILY-FRIENDLY   ○ GLUTEN FREE   ● LOW CAL   ● QUICK   ● FREEZABLE

★★★★★

A very satisfying soup. Great to beat the winter blues.
The tofu really makes the dish. **LARZA**

15 *minutes prep*

POTATO & SWISS CHEESE

Savoury soups are wow on the tastebuds! Make this cheesy concoction ahead of time and reheat for a quick and easy midweek meal.

SERVES 4 **PREP** 15 mins **COOK** 35 mins

½ cup watercress sprigs

125ml (½ cup) extra virgin olive oil, plus extra 2 tbs

1 brown onion, finely chopped

1.25kg desiree potatoes, peeled, chopped

1L (4 cups) chicken stock or vegetable stock

2 tsp finely chopped fresh rosemary

375ml (1½ cups) milk

150g (1½ cups) grated Swiss cheese

4 pieces short cut bacon, thinly sliced, fried

Finely chopped red onion, trimmed watercress sprigs and grilled cheesy toast (optional, see tip), to serve

1 Place the watercress and oil in a small food processor. Process until smooth. Strain through a very fine sieve into a jug. Set aside.

2 Heat 1 tbs extra oil in a large saucepan over medium-high heat. Add the onion. Cook, stirring, for 5 minutes or until softened. Stir in the potato. Increase heat to high. Add the stock and rosemary. Bring to the boil. Reduce heat to low and simmer, partially covered, for 15-20 minutes or until potato is tender.

3 Use a stick blender to blend soup in the pan until smooth. Place over medium-low heat. Add the milk. Cook, stirring, for 3 minutes or until heated through. Add the cheese and stir until smooth.

4 Ladle soup among serving bowls. Drizzle with watercress oil and remaining olive oil. Sprinkle with bacon, red onion, and watercress. Serve with toast, if you like.

COOK'S TIP

You can't have too much cheese! To make cheesy toast, cut very thin slices of your favourite crusty bread or baguette. Toast both sides under an oven grill. Sprinkle with grated Swiss cheese and grill until melted.

NUTRITION (PER SERVE)

CALS	FAT	SAT FAT	PROTEIN	CARBS
594	25g	13g	28g	38g

● EASY ● FAMILY-FRIENDLY ○ GLUTEN FREE ○ LOW CAL ○ QUICK ● FREEZABLE

ITALIAN STRACCIATELLA EGG

Popular in central Italy, this chicken soup features threads of egg. It's quick and easy to make – ideal for busy nights when there's barely time to cook!

SERVES 4 **PREP** 10 mins **COOK** 15 mins

- 1.5L (6 cups) gluten-free chicken stock
- 2 small zucchini, thinly sliced
- 150g (1 cup) frozen peas
- 150g pkt kale leaf and spinach
- 150g (1½ cups) shredded cooked chicken
- 2 green shallots, thinly sliced
- ½ cup fresh basil leaves, shredded
- 2 eggs
- 25g (⅓ cup) finely grated parmesan
- 2 tsp chilli-infused extra virgin olive oil
- Lemon wedges, to serve

1 Bring the stock to the boil in a large saucepan over high heat. Add zucchini. Cook, stirring, for 5 minutes or until almost tender. Add peas and leaf mixture. Cook, stirring, for 1 minute or until peas are just heated through. Add chicken, shallot and basil. Cook, stirring, for 1 minute or until chicken is heated through.

2 Meanwhile, whisk the eggs and parmesan in a small bowl (see tip). Slowly pour into stock mixture, stirring constantly, until the egg is just cooked (about 1 minute). Season. Drizzle with chilli oil. Serve with lemon wedges.

COOK'S TIP

If you're not serving this soup immediately, store the egg mixture in a small container and stir into the soup after reheating.

NUTRITION (PER SERVE)

CALS	FAT	SAT FAT	PROTEIN	CARBS
265	11g	84g	329.2g	9.6g

★★★★★

The quickest, easiest, tastiest soup recipe. **KATHIX**

● EASY ● FAMILY-FRIENDLY ● GLUTEN FREE ● LOW CAL ● QUICK ○ FREEZABLE

CHICKEN & VEG WITH CHILLI DRIZZLE

Fire up the tastebuds! We've given this nourishing chicken and vegetable soup a fiery chilli dressing for an exciting boost of flavour.

SERVES 4 **PREP** 20 mins **COOK** 20 mins

2 green zucchini, halved crossways
2 yellow zucchini, halved crossways
1 small (250g) narrow orange sweet
    potato, peeled, halved crossways
1 tbs extra virgin olive oil
2 green shallots, chopped
2 garlic cloves, crushed
1L (4 cups) gluten-free chicken stock
200g (2 cups) sliced cooked chicken
    (see tips)
Fresh coriander and Thai basil
    sprigs, plus lime cheeks, to serve

CHILLI DRIZZLE
4 small red chillies, halved
1 tbs extra virgin olive oil
2 tbs fresh coriander leaves
2 tbs fresh lime juice

1 Using the thin julienne setting on a vegetable spiraliser (see tips), cut the zucchini halves into 'noodles'. Using the thickest julienne setting on the spiraliser, cut the sweet potato halves into 'noodles'.

2 Heat the oil in a large saucepan over medium-high heat. Add the shallot and garlic. Cook, stirring, for 30 seconds or until just softened. Add the stock and 500ml (2 cups) water. Bring to the boil. Reduce the heat to low and simmer for 10 minutes.

3 Meanwhile, to make the chilli drizzle, place the chilli, oil, coriander and lime juice in a small food processor. Process until mixture is well combined. Season.

4 Add the chicken and the zucchini and sweet potato noodles to the soup. Season. Simmer for 5 minutes or until chicken is heated through.

5 Ladle soup among serving bowls. Top with the chilli drizzle, coriander and basil. Serve with lime cheeks.

COOK'S TIPS

If you don't have a spiraliser, simply cut the veg into thin matchsticks. We used poached chicken breast, but you can use barbecued chicken, if preferred.

NUTRITION (PER SERVE)

CALS	FAT	SAT FAT	PROTEIN	CARBS
291	15.1g	82.9g	21.5g	14.5g

● EASY ○ FAMILY-FRIENDLY ● GLUTEN FREE ● LOW CAL ○ QUICK ○ FREEZABLE

SPICY THAI PUMPKIN &
PRAWN

This scrumptious Thai soup will impress the family and any guests.
Enjoy the chunky veg before slurping up the spicy broth.

SERVES 4 **PREP** 15 mins **COOK** 25 mins

2 tbs vegetable oil
2 French shallots, thinly sliced
60g (¼ cup) Thai red curry paste
1L (4 cups) chicken stock
400g butternut pumpkin, peeled,
   cut into 2cm pieces
125g dried rice vermicelli noodles
800g medium green prawns, peeled,
   deveined, tails intact
400ml can light coconut milk
100g green beans, trimmed,
   cut into 3cm lengths
1 tbs fresh lime juice
Fresh Thai basil leaves, sliced red
   chilli and lime wedges, to serve

1 Heat the oil in a wok over medium heat. Add the French shallot and cook, stirring, for 1-2 minutes or until just golden. Using a slotted spoon, transfer to a plate lined with paper towel to drain. Increase heat to medium-high.

2 Add curry paste to the wok. Cook, stirring, for 1 minute or until aromatic. Pour in the stock and bring to the boil. Add the pumpkin. Reduce the heat to medium-low. Simmer for 5 minutes. Add the noodles. Cook, stirring occasionally, for 3 minutes.

3 Stir in the prawns. Cook for 4 minutes or until prawns become opaque and are just cooked through. Stir in the coconut milk and beans. Bring to a simmer. Cook for 2-3 minutes or until beans are tender. Stir in the lime juice.

4 Ladle the soup among serving bowls. Top with basil, chilli and French shallot. Serve with lime wedges.

COOK'S TIP

Swap the prawns
for 600g chopped
firm white fish
fillet, if you like.
Cook for 2 minutes
before adding
the coconut milk
and beans.

NUTRITION (PER SERVE)

CALS	FAT	SAT FAT	PROTEIN	CARBS
452	19.6g	8.6g	28.7g	41.4g

★★★★★

This was lovely; tasted like takeaway Thai. **VIOLAPARMESAN**

● **EASY** ○ FAMILY-FRIENDLY ○ GLUTEN FREE ○ LOW CAL ○ QUICK ○ FREEZABLE

SMOKY CHIPOTLE MEX
PUMPKIN

Pumpkin soup gets a Mexican makeover with a spicy kick and corn chip dippers. It's easy to make and freezes well, too.

SERVES 4 **PREP** 10 mins **COOK** 45 mins

80ml (⅓ cup) olive oil
1 red onion, finely chopped
2 garlic cloves, crushed
1½ tbs smoky chipotle seasoning
1 tsp ground cumin
1L (4 cups) chicken stock
1.5kg butternut pumpkin, peeled,
    deseeded, coarsely chopped
170g pkt corn chips
1 tsp smoked paprika,
    plus extra, to serve
100g (1 cup) coarsely grated
    jalapeño cheese
170g (⅔ cup) sour cream
2 jalapeños, sliced
Small fresh coriander leaves, to serve
2 tbs chipotle in adobo sauce

ROAST CAPSICUM
& BLACK BEAN SALSA

1 red capsicum, quartered,
    deseeded
½ small red onion, finely chopped
½ lime, juiced
125g can black beans, rinsed,
    drained

1 To make the salsa, heat a chargrill pan on medium-high. Grill the capsicum, skin-side down, for 4-5 minutes or until all skin is charred. Cool slightly then chop into 1cm pieces. Transfer to a bowl. Add the onion, lime juice and black beans. Toss until well combined. Season well.

2 Meanwhile, heat oil in a large saucepan over medium heat. Add onion. Cook, stirring, for 5 minutes or until softened. Add garlic, chipotle seasoning and cumin. Cook, stirring, for 1 minute or until aromatic. Pour in stock. Bring to the boil. Add pumpkin. Reduce the heat to medium-low. Simmer for 25 minutes or until pumpkin is tender. Remove from heat.

3 Meanwhile, preheat an oven grill on medium. Place corn chips on a baking tray. Sprinkle with paprika and cheese. Grill for 2-3 minutes or until cheese is melted and golden.

4 Use a stick blender to blend soup until smooth. Place over low heat for 10 minutes or until thickened slightly.

5 Ladle soup among serving bowls. Swirl soup with half the sour cream. Arrange corn chips on 1 side of soup. Top with salsa, jalapeño and coriander. Dollop with remaining sour cream. Drizzle with chipotle sauce. Sprinkle with extra paprika, to serve.

COOK'S TIP

If you prefer to ease up on the chilli and make this more kid-friendly, reduce the chipotle seasoning to 2 tsp, use regular cheddar instead of jalapeño cheese, and omit the jalapeños and chipotle in adobo sauce.

NUTRITION (PER SERVE)

CALS	FAT	SAT FAT	PROTEIN	CARBS
869	57g	23g	21g	60g

● EASY ● FAMILY-FRIENDLY ○ GLUTEN FREE ○ LOW CAL ○ QUICK ● FREEZABLE

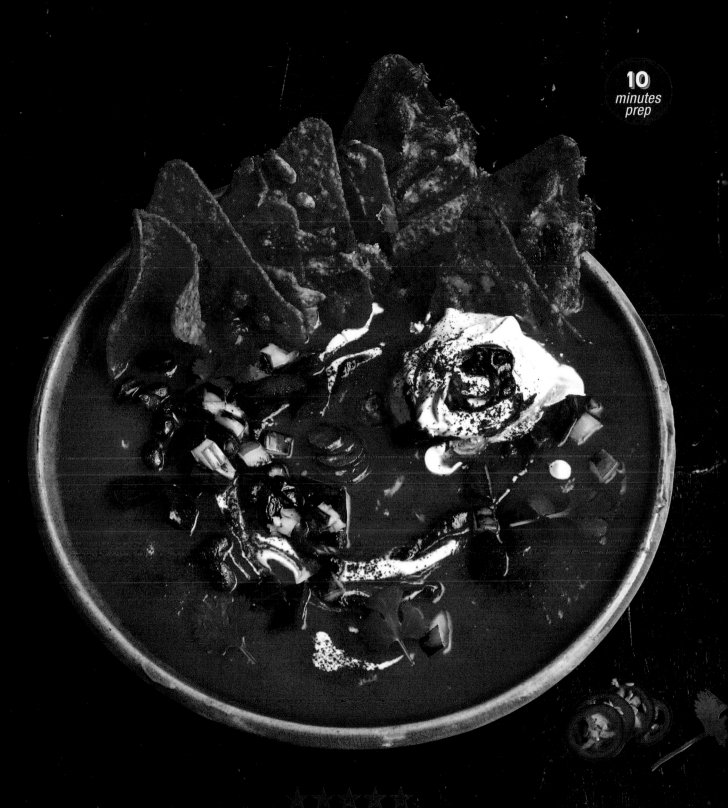

*I never thought I'd enjoy a pumpkin soup, but this was delicious!
It was so good I'm cooking it again this week.* **BECCIEBLOSSOM**

PASTA & NOODLES

LOADED SOUPS DELIVER A FULFILLING BOWL. THESE ARE ALL HEAVENLY, AND MANY ARE GLUTEN-FREE, TOO.

HEALTHY CHICKEN NOODLE

Full of nutrient-dense vegies, such as broccolini and buk choy, plus chicken thighs for iron, this hearty Asian-inspired soup is good for the body and soul!

SERVES 4 **PREP** 20 mins **COOK** 30 mins

100g dried rice vermicelli noodles

2 tsp macadamia oil

1 large brown onion, finely chopped

2 large celery sticks, finely chopped

2 garlic cloves, crushed

3cm-piece fresh ginger,
    peeled, thinly sliced

1 long fresh red chilli, deseeded,
    finely chopped

1 lemongrass stem, trimmed,
    cut into 4cm lengths, bruised

400g chicken thigh fillets,
    fat trimmed

500ml (2 cups) gluten-free
    chicken stock

250g cherry tomatoes, halved

1 bunch broccolini, cut into
    4cm lengths

150g snow peas, thinly sliced

1 bunch baby buk choy, cut into
    4cm lengths

1 tbs fresh lime juice

Fresh Thai basil leaves, to serve

1 Place the noodles in a large heatproof bowl. Cover with boiling water. Set aside for 5 minutes to soften. Drain.

2 Heat the oil in a large saucepan over medium heat. Add the onion and celery. Cook, stirring, for 5-6 minutes or until softened. Add the garlic, ginger, chilli and lemongrass. Cook, stirring, for 1 minute or until aromatic. Add the chicken and cook for 1 minute or until starting to change colour.

3 Pour in the stock and 750ml (3 cups) water. Bring to the boil. Reduce heat to low. Simmer, partially covered, for 10 minutes or until the chicken is cooked through. Use tongs to transfer chicken to a clean board. Cool slightly. Shred. Return chicken to pan.

4 Add the tomato, broccolini and snow peas to the soup. Simmer for 3-4 minutes or until vegetables are just tender. Stir through buk choy until just wilted. Stir in lime juice and season. Divide noodles among serving bowls. Ladle over the soup. Top with basil, to serve.

COOK'S NOTE

Add any Asian greens you like to this soup. You can also swap the broccolini for broccoli florets, and the cherry tomatoes for canned cherry tomatoes.

NUTRITION (PER SERVE)

CALS	FAT	SAT FAT	PROTEIN	CARBS
290	7.5g	1.5g	23g	27.5g

● EASY ● FAMILY-FRIENDLY ● GLUTEN FREE ● LOW CAL ○ QUICK ○ FREEZABLE

★★★★★
Easy to make. Tastes sooo good. Added a few fresh herbs, as well. Eat with crusty bread – perfecto! **KATT3**

20 minutes prep

79

CREAMY TORTELLINI
MINESTRONE

Nothing says winter comfort food like a pasta, soup and cream combo. This twist on the classic minestrone is one to remember.

SERVES 4 **PREP** 15 mins **COOK** 20 mins

2 tbs olive oil
100g pancetta, coarsely chopped
2 carrots, peeled, finely chopped
2 celery sticks, finely chopped
1 brown onion, finely chopped
2 garlic cloves, crushed
1L (4 cups) chicken stock
400g can diced Italian tomatoes
325g pkt spinach and ricotta
   tortellini
400g can borlotti beans,
   rinsed, drained
80g (⅔ cup) crème fraîche
75g (¼ cup) bought basil pesto
Fresh small basil leaves, to serve

1 Heat the oil in a large saucepan over medium-high heat. Add the pancetta, carrot, celery and onion. Cook, stirring often, for 5-8 minutes or until the vegetables are softened. Add the garlic and cook, stirring, for 30 seconds or until aromatic.

2 Add the stock and tomato to the pan. Bring mixture to the boil. Add the tortellini and borlotti beans. Cover and return to a gentle simmer. Uncover and reduce the heat to medium. Cook, stirring often, for 2-3 minutes or until the tortellini is al dente.

3 Ladle the minestrone among serving bowls. Top with a dollop of the crème fraîche and the pesto. Sprinkle with the basil, to serve.

COOK'S NOTE

Swap the crème fraîche for sour cream, if you like.

NUTRITION (PER SERVE)

CALS	FAT	SAT FAT	PROTEIN	CARBS
672	43.4g	17g	22.2g	45.6g

★★★★★

Everyone in the family enjoyed this meal. I couldn't source crème fraîche, so I used sour cream and it was beautiful. **HAYLEYPO39**

● EASY ● FAMILY-FRIENDLY ○ GLUTEN FREE ○ LOW CAL ○ QUICK ○ FREEZABLE

ONE-POT SPAGHETTI & MEATBALL

Spaghetti and ready-made meatballs get turned into a one-pot soup in this quick and easy dinner idea that's on the table in 45 minutes.

SERVES 4 **PREP** 10 mins **COOK** 35 mins

1 tbs extra virgin olive oil
400g pkt beef and lamb meatballs
1 small brown onion, finely chopped
1 carrot, finely chopped
2 celery stalks, finely chopped
1 garlic clove, crushed
500ml (2 cups) chicken stock
500g jar tomato pasta sauce
150g spaghetti, broken in half
40g (⅓ cup) pre-grated mozzarella
Finely grated parmesan, small
   fresh basil leaves and garlic
   bread, to serve

1 Heat the oil in a large, heavy-based saucepan over medium-high heat. Cook the meatballs, turning occasionally, for 5 minutes or until browned all over. Transfer to a plate.

2 Add the onion to the pan. Cook, stirring occasionally, for 5 minutes or until softened. Add the carrot, celery and garlic. Cook for 5 minutes or until the vegetables are tender.

3 Return meatballs to the pan with the stock and pasta sauce. Bring to a simmer. Cook, stirring occasionally, for 10 minutes. Add spaghetti. Cook for 8-10 minutes or until spaghetti is al dente and meatballs are cooked. Season.

4 Ladle soup among serving bowls. Top with mozzarella, parmesan and basil. Season. Serve with garlic bread.

COOK'S NOTE

Experiment with different flavoured meatballs, if you desire. Try, pork, chicken or veal.

NUTRITION (PER SERVE)

CALS	FAT	SAT FAT	PROTEIN	CARBS
677	34.8g	15.8g	29.4g	58.3g

★★★★★

I had most of the ingredients for this already, so decided to give it a go. It was great! Really easy and tasty. **FOODSLED**

● EASY ● FAMILY-FRIENDLY ○ GLUTEN FREE ○ LOW CAL ○ QUICK ○ FREEZABLE

ONE-POT CHEESY LASAGNE

With a tomato broth and fresh herbs, this amazing soup has all the delicious flavours of lasagne. It's set to be on high rotation on your menu!

SERVES 4 **PREP** 15 mins **COOK** 45 mins

1 tbs extra virgin olive oil

1 brown onion, finely chopped

400g beef mince

2 garlic cloves, crushed

2 tbs plain flour

2 tbs tomato paste

500g jar tomato pasta sauce

1L (4 cups) chicken stock

5 dried lasagne sheets

2 tbs milk

2 tbs chopped fresh continental parsley leaves, plus extra, to serve

2 tbs chopped fresh basil leaves, plus extra, to serve

55g (½ cup) grated mozzarella

20g (¼ cup) finely grated parmesan

1 Heat the oil in a large, heavy-based saucepan over medium-high heat. Add the onion. Cook for 5 minutes or until softened. Add the beef. Cook, breaking up mince with a wooden spoon, for 6-8 minutes or until browned. Add garlic. Cook for 1 minute or until aromatic. Stir in the flour and tomato paste. Add the pasta sauce and stock. Bring to the boil. Reduce heat to low. Simmer, stirring occasionally, for 15 minutes or until thickened slightly.

2 Break the lasagne sheets into 6cm pieces. Add to the soup. Simmer, stirring occasionally, for 10 minutes or until pasta is just tender. Add the milk, parsley and basil. Season. Stir to combine.

3 Ladle soup among serving bowls. Top with mozzarella, parmesan, and the extra parsley and basil. Serve.

COOK'S TIP

You could use any shape of dried pasta you have on hand for this recipe.

NUTRITION (PER SERVE)

CALS	FAT	SAT FAT	PROTEIN	CARBS
503	19.8g	8.3g	38.5g	40g

★★★★★ *LOVED this soup. So easy and tasty, and all in one pot.* **SHEVAUN39**

● EASY ● FAMILY-FRIENDLY ○ GLUTEN FREE ○ LOW CAL ○ QUICK ○ FREEZABLE

15
minutes
prep

85

SLOW COOKER PORK BELLY
RAMEN

Making ramen at home is easier than it seems, especially with a slow cooker. Our recipe uses melt-in-your-mouth pork belly and creamy soft-boiled eggs.

SERVES 4 **PREP** 10 mins **COOK** 6 hours 20 mins

1 tbs peanut oil
1kg boneless pork belly roast
1 garlic bulb, halved horizontally
1.25L (5 cups) chicken stock
5cm-piece fresh ginger,
    thickly sliced
1 green shallot, halved, plus extra,
    sliced diagonally, to serve
2 tbs mirin
2 tbs light soy sauce
1 tsp sambal oelek (see tip)
200g dried ramen noodles
2 cups baby spinach
4 eggs, soft-boiled, halved
    crossways
Sliced fresh red chilli, to serve
    (optional)

1 Heat the oil in a large frying pan. Add the pork, rind-side down, and cook for 10 minutes or until golden. Turn over and cook for a further 5 minutes, adding the garlic, cut-side down, in the last 2 minutes of cooking. Transfer the pork and garlic to a slow cooker. Add the stock, ginger and shallot. Cover and cook on High for 5-6 hours or until the pork is very tender.

2 Use tongs to transfer the pork to a plate. Cool slightly. Remove and discard the rind and fat. Use forks to coarsely shred the pork and transfer to a baking tray.

3 Stir the mirin, soy sauce and sambal oelek into the slow cooker, adding a little more to taste, if desired.

4 Cook the noodles in a large saucepan of boiling water for 5 minutes or until just tender. Drain and divide among serving bowls.

5 Meanwhile, preheat an oven grill on high. Place the pork under the grill for 3 minutes or until browned.

6 Divide the pork and spinach among the bowls. Pour in the broth. Serve topped with egg halves, extra shallot and the chilli, if using.

COOK'S TIP

Sambal oelek is an Indonesian chilli paste made with red chilli, vinegar and a little salt. You can substitute with sriracha, if you like.

NUTRITION (PER SERVE)

CALS	FAT	SAT FAT	PROTEIN	CARBS
503	19.8g	8.3g	38.5g	40g

● EASY ○ FAMILY-FRIENDLY ○ GLUTEN FREE ○ LOW CAL ○ QUICK ○ FREEZABLE

10
minutes
prep

★★★★★
We make this ramen all
the time. It's so delicious.
I've tried a few different
versions, but always come
back to this one. **STEPH_2103**

QUICK THAI RED CHICKEN CURRY

A bowl of warming noodles is just minutes away with this spicy chicken noodle soup packed with lots of wholesome fresh veg.

SERVES 4 **PREP** 10 mins **COOK** 10 mins

2 cooked chicken breasts
1 tbs canola oil
1 tbs gluten-free red curry paste
1L (4 cups) gluten-free chicken stock
400ml can coconut milk
3 kaffir lime leaves
100g snow peas, thinly sliced
   lengthways
6 canned baby corn spears,
   halved lengthways
100g dried rice vermicelli noodles
2 tsp fish sauce
2 small fresh red chillies, sliced
2 fresh coriander sprigs,
   leaves picked
1 fresh lime, cut into wedges

1 Heat a large, deep frying pan over high heat and bring a small saucepan of water to the boil.

2 Shred the chicken, discarding any skin. Add the oil and curry paste to the frying pan and cook, stirring, for 30 seconds or until aromatic. Add the stock, coconut milk and 2 lime leaves. Bring to the boil.

3 Meanwhile, add the snow peas and corn to the boiling water and cook for 2-3 minutes or until tender-crisp.

4 Finely slice remaining lime leaf. Add noodles to the stock mixture. Cook for 2 minutes or until noodles soften. Stir in the chicken and fish sauce. Ladle soup among serving bowls and top with snow peas, corn, chilli, sliced lime leaf and coriander. Serve with lime wedges.

COOK'S TIP

For a simple seafood curry, swap the chicken for 400g marinara mix. Add to the stock with the noodles.

NUTRITION (PER SERVE)

CALS	FAT	SAT FAT	PROTEIN	CARBS
461	25.2g	14.6g	30.9g	25.1g

● EASY ○ FAMILY-FRIENDLY ● GLUTEN FREE ○ LOW CAL ● QUICK ○ FREEZABLE

RACY JAPANESE TOFU
RAMEN

Enjoy a delicious vegetarian ramen soup quicker than you can find the chopsticks, using our few easy shortcuts.

SERVES 4 **PREP** 5 mins **COOK** 10 mins

1L (4 cups) vegetable stock
1 tbs miso paste
2 tsp sesame seeds
1 tbs vegetable oil
200g pkt Japanese-marinated tofu
2 baby buk choy
250g pkt sweet potato noodles
250g pkt zucchini noodles
4 x 150g pkt shelf-fresh
   ramen noodles
Soy sauce, to taste

1 Combine the stock and 500ml (2 cups) water in a large saucepan. Cover. Bring to the boil over high heat. Reduce heat to low and stir in the miso.

2 Meanwhile, cook the sesame seeds in a frying pan over medium-high heat for 1-2 minutes or until toasted. Transfer to a bowl. Heat the oil in the same pan. Cook tofu for 1 minute each side or until browned. Transfer to a board. Cut into cubes. Cut buk choy into quarters lengthways.

3 Add the buk choy, plus the sweet potato and zucchini noodles, to the pan. Heat for 2 minutes or until the vegetables are just softened. Divide ramen noodles among serving bowls. Ladle over some hot broth. Set aside for 1 minute to soften and then use a fork to loosen ramen.

4 Divide the buk choy, vegie noodles and remaining broth among the bowls. Top with the tofu and sesame seeds. Season with soy sauce, to serve.

COOK'S TIP

You'll find different-flavoured marinated tofu at the supermarket. Change it up for a spicier version, if you prefer.

NUTRITION (PER SERVE)

CALS	FAT	SAT FAT	PROTEIN	CARBS
444	14.5g	2.2g	21.2g	53g

★★★★★ *Delicious and simple to cook at home.* **SUSIE1997**

● EASY ○ FAMILY-FRIENDLY ○ GLUTEN FREE ● LOW CAL ● QUICK ○ FREEZABLE

INDONESIAN RICE & NOODLE CHICKEN

Also known as *soto ayam*, this spicy chicken noodle soup is packed with chicken and zesty flavours. It's a mighty fine meal for all.

SERVES 4 **PREP** 20 mins **COOK** 1 hour 25 mins

5cm-piece fresh ginger, peeled, chopped
4 garlic cloves, chopped
½ red onion, chopped
1 long fresh red chilli, chopped
1 tbs peanut oil
1 tsp ground turmeric
8 (about 1kg) chicken drumsticks
750ml (3 cups) gluten-free chicken stock
1 lemongrass stem, bruised
3 fresh kaffir limes leaves
200g dried rice vermicelli noodles
Halved hard-boiled eggs, sambal oelek, thinly sliced green shallots, fried shallots, fresh bean sprouts and fresh coriander leaves, to serve

1 Process the ginger, garlic, onion and chilli in a small food processor, adding 1 tbs water if needed, to form a smooth paste.

2 Heat the oil in a large saucepan over medium heat. Add the ginger paste and turmeric. Cook, stirring often, for 5 minutes or until aromatic. Add the chicken and turn to coat. Add the stock, 750ml (3 cups) water, lemongrass and lime leaves. Season well with salt. Reduce the heat to low and simmer, uncovered, for 1¼ hours or until the meat is falling off the bones. Transfer chicken to a plate. Set aside for 5 minutes to cool slightly. Remove meat from the bones, discarding skin and bones. Coarsely chop the meat.

3 Meanwhile, place the noodles in a heatproof bowl. Cover with boiling water. Set aside for 20 minutes to soften. Drain well.

4 Remove and discard the lemongrass from the broth. Divide noodles among serving bowls. Top with the chicken. Ladle over the broth. Top with egg, sambal oelek, shallot, fried shallots, bean sprouts and coriander. Serve.

COOK'S TIP

Not a fan of a lot of chilli? Simply remove the seeds from the fresh chilli before processing, and go easy on the sambal oelek (or omit) when serving.

NUTRITION (PER SERVE)

CALS	FAT	SAT FAT	PROTEIN	CARBS
504	18.1g	4.5g	41.8g	41.6g

○ EASY ○ FAMILY-FRIENDLY ● GLUTEN FREE ○ LOW CAL ○ QUICK ○ FREEZABLE

Lots of flavour; really yum! MIK1111

PUMPKIN CURRY NOODLE

We've turned pumpkin soup into an Asian-style broth with noodles – complete with fresh vegies, spices and coconut milk. It's wonderfully creamy.

SERVES 4 **PREP** 10 mins **COOK** 35 mins

1 tbs coconut oil
800g pkt diced pumpkin
1 red capsicum, coarsely chopped
2 garlic cloves, coarsely chopped
⅓ bunch fresh coriander, root and stems finely chopped, leaves reserved
4 green shallots, thinly sliced diagonally
100g (⅓ cup) vegan Thai red curry paste
400ml can coconut milk
500ml (2 cups) plant-based chicken stock (see tip)
2-3 tsp soy sauce, to taste
3 tsp brown sugar
1 lime, halved
100g dried brown rice vermicelli noodles
Toasted pepitas, to serve

1 Heat the oil in a large saucepan over medium heat. Add the pumpkin, capsicum, garlic, coriander root and stem, and white section of the shallot. Cook, stirring occasionally, for 6 minutes or until pumpkin is starting to soften. Add the curry paste and cook, stirring, for 2 minutes or until aromatic.

2 Add the coconut milk and stock. Bring to the boil. Simmer, covered, stirring occasionally, for 20 minutes or until vegies are just soft. Stir in the soy sauce, sugar and juice of 1 lime half. Use a stick blender to the puree mixture in the pan until smooth.

3 Meanwhile, cook the noodles in a large saucepan of boiling water for 5 minutes or until tender. Drain. Refresh under cold running water. Drain well. Divide soup among serving bowls. Top with the noodles. Sprinkle with reserved coriander leaves, green section of shallot and pepitas. Serve with remaining lime cut into wedges.

COOK'S TIP

Many bought stocks and stock powders are vegetarian, and are only flavoured as "chicken" or "beef" using plant-based products. Check the label before buying.

NUTRITION (PER SERVE)

CALS	FAT	SAT FAT	PROTEIN	CARBS
451	24g	17.3g	11.2g	44.8g

★★★★★ *Love it; will be making again!* **HANNAHODONNELL**

● EASY ● FAMILY-FRIENDLY ○ GLUTEN FREE ○ LOW CAL ○ QUICK ○ FREEZABLE

JAPANESE SALMON NOODLE CURRY

Dinner's on the table in 30 minutes with this easy-peasy Japanese-inspired curry noodle soup. Just the thing for busier nights.

SERVES 4 **PREP** 10 mins **COOK** 15 mins

2 tbs olive oil

1 brown onion, cut into thin wedges

1 carrot, peeled, cut into noodles using a julienne peeler (see tip)

1L (4 cups) chicken stock

4 (about 180g each) skinless salmon fillets

1 tbs dark soy sauce

440g pkt shelf-fresh udon noodles

1 bunch baby buk choy, halved

92g pkt mild golden curry sauce mix

2 green shallots, thinly sliced

Sesame seeds, toasted, to serve

1 Heat 1 tbs oil in a large saucepan over high heat. Add onion and carrot. Cook, stirring occasionally, for 3 minutes or until onion is soft. Add stock and 1L (4 cups) water. Cover. Bring to boil. Reduce heat to medium. Simmer for 5 minutes or until carrot is just tender. Transfer carrot to a bowl.

2 Meanwhile, place salmon in a shallow dish. Rub all over with 3 tsp soy sauce. Heat remaining oil in a large non-stick frying pan over medium-high heat. Add salmon and cook for 3 minutes on each side or until just cooked through. Transfer to a plate. Cover to keep warm.

3 Place noodles in a heatproof bowl. Cover with boiling water. Set aside for 2 minutes to soften. Drain.

4 Add the buk choy and curry mix to the stock mixture. Stir for 1 minute or until the curry mix dissolves. Stir in the remaining soy sauce and season.

5 Divide noodles, buk choy and soup among serving bowls. Top with salmon and carrot. Sprinkle with shallot and sesame seeds, to serve.

COOK'S TIP

If you don't have a julienne peeler, simply cut the carrot into thin matchsticks.

NUTRITION (PER SERVE)

CALS	FAT	SAT FAT	PROTEIN	CARBS
826	48.4g	13g	48.5g	46.7g

● EASY ○ FAMILY-FRIENDLY ○ GLUTEN FREE ○ LOW CAL ● QUICK ○ FREEZABLE

★★★★★ *We really enjoyed this soup. It was filling, the salmon was cooked perfectly and the broth was wow.* **MURRAYMINT**

CREAMY CHICKEN NOODLE

This comforting one-pot soup is full of nourishing ingredients, including chicken and ginger, plus it's low-calorie to boot.

SERVES 4 **PREP** 15 mins **COOK** 40 mins

100g dried rice vermicelli noodles

2 tsp extra virgin olive oil

2 (about 400g) small chicken breast fillets

4cm-piece fresh ginger, peeled, cut into thin matchsticks

2 garlic cloves, crushed

2 tbs gluten-free yellow curry paste

400g sweet potato, peeled, cut into 1.5cm pieces

1.5L (6 cups) salt-reduced, gluten-free chicken stock

270ml can light coconut cream

1 tbs gluten-free light soy sauce

½ wombok (Chinese cabbage), thinly shredded

2 green shallots, trimmed, very finely sliced

Fresh coriander sprigs and sliced long fresh red chilli (optional), to serve

1 Place the noodles in a heatproof bowl. Pour over enough boiling water to cover. Set aside for 5-7 minutes or until tender. Drain.

2 Meanwhile, heat the oil in a wok over medium-high heat. Season the chicken and cook for 6 minutes on each side or until cooked through. Transfer to a plate and cover with foil to keep warm.

3 Add the ginger and garlic to the wok. Cook, stirring, for 1 minute or until softened. Add the curry paste and cook, stirring, for 30 seconds or until aromatic. Add the sweet potato, stock and coconut cream. Bring to the boil. Reduce the heat to low and simmer for 15-20 minutes or until the sweet potato is very tender. Stir in the soy sauce.

4 Meanwhile, slice the chicken. Divide the cabbage and noodles among serving bowls. Ladle in the soup. Top with chicken, shallot, coriander and chilli, if using. Serve.

COOK'S TIP

For a vegetarian version, replace the chicken with sliced and pan-fried tofu. Go further and make it vegan by using a vegan curry paste.

NUTRITION (PER SERVE)

CALS	FAT	SAT FAT	PROTEIN	CARBS
388	12.5g	7g	28g	38g

● EASY ○ FAMILY-FRIENDLY ● GLUTEN FREE ● LOW CAL ○ QUICK ○ FREEZABLE

15
minutes
prep

CHICKEN, BACON &
VERMICELLI

A quick soup to make and slurp up on midweek nights – we bet you already have most of the ingredients in the house.

SERVES 4 **PREP** 10 mins **COOK** 20 mins

2 tbs olive oil

200g bought diced bacon

1 brown onion, finely chopped

500g chicken breast fillets, cut into 2cm pieces

140g (½ cup) tomato paste

400g can cannellini beans, rinsed, drained

400g can creamed corn

10 fresh thyme sprigs, plus extra, to serve

1L (4 cups) gluten-free chicken stock

125g dried rice vermicelli noodles

Finely grated parmesan, to serve

1 Heat 1 tbs oil in a large saucepan over high heat. Add the bacon and cook, stirring, for 3-4 minutes or until crispy. Transfer to a plate.

2 Heat the remaining oil in the pan over medium-high heat. Add the onion and chicken. Cook, stirring, for 6 minutes or until golden and cooked through. Add tomato paste, beans, corn, thyme and stock. Season. Cover. Bring to the boil.

3 Add the vermicelli to the chicken mixture and cook for 6 minutes or until softened. Divide soup among serving bowls. Top with bacon, extra thyme and parmesan, to serve.

NUTRITION (PER SERVE)

CALS	FAT	SAT FAT	PROTEIN	CARBS
648	23.3g	6.9g	50.1g	53.4g

COOK'S TIP

Cannellini beans can be replaced with red kidney beans or four bean mix – whatever you have on hand. No vermicelli? Use linguine or angel hair pasta – gluten-free, if necessary.

● EASY ● FAMILY-FRIENDLY ● GLUTEN FREE ○ LOW CAL ● QUICK ○ FREEZABLE

★★★★★

Loved this recipe; held up in the fridge, too! **TVITT**

SPEEDY TUSCAN TORTELLINI

Simple but flavourful, this soup will soon become a staple in your household. And you'll just love the added spiciness of the Italian sausage.

SERVES 4 **PREP** 5 mins **COOK** 10 mins

1 tbs olive oil

3 Italian sausages (see tip)

800g can diced tomatoes

1L (4 cups) chicken stock

325g pkt basil and pine nuts pesto tortellini

400g can red kidney beans, rinsed, drained

80g baby spinach

Pre-grated parmesan, to serve

1 Heat the oil in a frying pan over medium-high heat. Add the sausages. Cover. Cook, turning occasionally, for 5 minutes or until just cooked.

2 Meanwhile, combine the tomato and stock in a large saucepan over high heat. Cover. Bring to the boil.

3 Add the tortellini and kidney beans to the tomato mixture. Simmer for 4 minutes or until pasta is al dente. Season.

4 Slice the sausages and add to the tomato mixture. Add the spinach and stir until wilted. Ladle soup among serving bowls. Sprinkle with parmesan, season and serve.

COOK'S TIP

Italian sausages are available at your local butcher. Any spicy sausage can be used instead.

NUTRITION (PER SERVE)

CALS	FAT	SAT FAT	PROTEIN	CARBS
617	33g	11.3g	32.1g	43.4g

★★★★★

It is a quick and easy soup, and really delicious considering no spices/herbs required. **JENIMARIE**

● EASY ● FAMILY-FRIENDLY ○ GLUTEN FREE ○ LOW CAL ● QUICK ○ FREEZABLE

SLOW COOKER CHICKEN LAKSA

Using a slow cooker to cook a laksa is the ideal at-home cheat. Time allows the soup to develop rich flavours and the result is mouth-watering.

SERVES 4 **PREP** 20 mins **COOK** 4 hours 5 mins

3 chicken thigh fillets, trimmed
120g (½ cup) bought gluten-free laksa paste
6 kaffir lime leaves, coarsely torn
2 lemongrass stems, trimmed, bruised
1L (4 cups) gluten-free chicken stock
400ml can coconut cream
400ml can coconut milk
150g green beans, trimmed, cut into thirds
200g dried rice vermicelli noodles
2 tbs fresh lime juice
1 cup bean sprouts, trimmed
1 small red chilli, thinly sliced
⅔ cup fresh coriander sprigs
Lime wedges, to serve

1 Combine the chicken and laksa paste in a slow cooker. Cook on High, turning chicken occasionally, for 5 minutes. Add the lime leaves, lemongrass, stock and coconut cream. Cover and cook on High for 3½ hours (or Low for 6 hours), or until chicken is cooked through.

2 Remove and discard lemongrass and lime leaves. Transfer chicken to a board. Using 2 forks, shred chicken. Return chicken to soup with coconut milk, beans and vermicelli. Season. Cook on High for 30 minutes or until the noodles have softened. Stir in the lime juice.

3 Divide laksa among serving bowls. Top with bean sprouts, chilli and coriander. Serve with lime wedges.

COOK'S TIP

You can cook this soup in a large heavy-based stockpot on the stovetop, if you prefer. Just ensure you cook the soup over low heat for 6 hours or it will burn in the pan.

NUTRITION (PER SERVE)

CALS	FAT	SAT FAT	PROTEIN	CARBS
846.6	52.2g	35.3g	31.2g	59.3g

★★★★★ *This is so delicious!* **SWANSGIRL22**

● EASY ○ FAMILY-FRIENDLY ● GLUTEN FREE ○ LOW CAL ○ QUICK ○ FREEZABLE

CHICKEN NOODLE CUPPA SOUP

Not much beats a mug of hot soup on chilly days, especially when it's a low-fat and wholesome – but still easy – alternative to a packet mix.

SERVES 1 **PREP** 5 mins **COOK** 5 mins

20g dried egg noodles
125g can creamed corn
25g (¼ cup) shredded cooked chicken
1 tsp chicken stock powder
Soy sauce, to season
Shaoxing wine (Chinese cooking wine), to season
Sesame oil, to season
Green shallots, sliced, to serve

1 Place the noodles in a 430ml (1¾ cup) mug. Add 250ml (1 cup) water. Microwave for 4 minutes or until the noodles are tender.

2 Stir in the corn, chicken and stock powder. Microwave for 30 seconds. Season with a dash of soy sauce and cooking wine, a few drops of sesame oil and pepper. Sprinkle with shallot, to serve.

COOK'S TIP

Swap the chicken for the same amount of shredded ham, if you like.

NUTRITION (PER SERVE)

CALS	FAT	SAT FAT	PROTEIN	CARBS
268	5.2g	1.1g	15.6g	36.6g

★★★★★

My kids love this! It's so quick and easy, and is a great lunch in winter. **SHAWNTHEPRAWN**

● EASY ● FAMILY-FRIENDLY ○ GLUTEN FREE ● LOW CAL ● QUICK ○ FREEZABLE

JAPANESE CHICKEN RAMEN

The perfect last-minute soup! Super quick to prepare and cook, this ramen will become your family go-to for busy evenings.

SERVES 4 **PREP** 10 mins **COOK** 10 mins

30g pkt Japanese instant miso soup mix
375ml (1½ cups) vegetable stock
3cm-piece ginger, peeled, cut into matchsticks
150g (1 cup) podded frozen edamame
4 x 120g ramen noodle cakes
2 barbecued chicken breasts
Lightly dried chilli flakes and toasted sesame seeds, to serve

1 Fill a kettle with water and bring to the boil. Empty the 3 sachets of miso soup into a large saucepan. Add the stock, ginger and 500ml (2 cups) tap water. Cover. Bring to the boil over high heat.

2 Meanwhile, fill a large saucepan one-quarter of the way with tap water. Add the boiling water. Cover and bring to the boil.

3 Add the edamame to the stock mixture and cook for 2 minutes or until just tender. Add the noodles to the boiling water. Cook for 2 minutes or until just tender. Drain.

4 Thinly slice the chicken breast. Divide the noodles among serving bowls. Ladle the soup mixture over the top. Top with the chicken. Sprinkle with the chilli and sesame seeds, to serve.

COOK'S TIP

You can buy barbecued chicken breasts from a takeaway chicken shop, or simply remove the breasts from a whole barbecued chicken.

NUTRITION (PER SERVE)

CALS	FAT	SAT FAT	PROTEIN	CARBS
839	35.2g	13.7g	46.9g	77.6g

★★★★★ *This is goooooooood! It's fast and easy. I have made this for the fam-squad quite a few times now.* **BBBBBB**

● EASY ● FAMILY-FRIENDLY ○ GLUTEN FREE ○ LOW CAL ● QUICK ○ FREEZABLE

CHICKEN, MISO & GINGER

This easy Japanese twist on the classic chicken soup is on the table in 25 minutes, and is full of flu-fighting goodness.

SERVES 4 **PREP** 10 mins **COOK** 15 mins

- 180g dried ramen noodles
- 1L (4 cups) chicken stock
- 2 bunches broccolini, trimmed
- 6cm-piece ginger, peeled, cut into thin matchsticks
- 75g (¼ cup) red miso paste
- 200g (2 cups) shredded barbecued chicken
- 200g enoki mushrooms
- 2 green shallots, thinly sliced
- 1 sheet nori, torn (optional)

1 Cook the noodles in a saucepan of boiling water following packet directions. Drain. Divide among 4 serving bowls.

2 Meanwhile, bring stock to the boil in a saucepan over high heat. Add the broccolini and ginger. Cook for 2 minutes or until broccolini is tender-crisp. Use tongs to divide broccolini among serving bowls.

3 Place the miso paste in a small heatproof bowl. Add a little of the stock, stirring until miso dissolves.

4 Add the miso mixture to the stock mixture and gently stir to combine. Bring to a simmer. Remove from heat. Arrange chicken and mushrooms in bowls. Ladle over miso mixture. Sprinkle with shallot and nori, if using. Serve.

COOK'S TIP

Nori is dried edible seaweed. You can buy it in sheets at supermarkets. Nori is a good source of omega-3 fatty acids, plus B and K vitamins.

NUTRITION (PER SERVE)

CALS	FAT	SAT FAT	PROTEIN	CARBS
564	16.3g	8g	25.3g	75.8g

★★★★★ *Amazingly easy. I poached the chicken in the soup and added bok choi. Delish!* **KMDUNC**

● EASY ○ FAMILY-FRIENDLY ○ GLUTEN FREE ○ LOW CAL ● QUICK ○ FREEZABLE

GREEN CURRY & BROCCOLI

A low-cal speedy and spicy Thai soup packed with nutritious broccoli. We loooove how the florets soak up the broth. Yummy!

SERVES 4 **PREP** 10 mins **COOK** 30 mins

1 large head broccoli, trimmed
2 tbs gluten-free Thai green
   curry paste
625ml (2½ cups) gluten-free
   chicken stock
2 potatoes, peeled, chopped
400ml can coconut milk
150g dried rice stick noodles
2 tbs fresh lime juice
Fresh coriander leaves and
   diagonally sliced green shallot,
   to serve

1 Remove large stems from the broccoli head and thinly slice. Cut remaining broccoli into small florets.

2 Heat a large heavy-based saucepan over medium-high heat. Add curry paste. Cook, stirring, for 2 minutes or until aromatic. Gradually stir in the stock until combined. Add 500ml (2 cups) water, the potato, broccoli stems and half the broccoli florets. Cover. Bring to the boil. Reduce heat to low. Simmer for 10-12 minutes or until potato is tender. Remove from the heat.

3 Use a stick blender to blend soup in pan until smooth. Place pan over a medium heat. Add remaining broccoli, plus the coconut milk and noodles. Season. Simmer, uncovered, for 8 minutes or until noodles are tender. Stir in lime juice. Top with coriander and shallot, to serve.

COOK'S TIP

Want this soup a little meatier? Just add 400g chopped firm white fish or chicken thigh fillet with the broccoli in step 3.

NUTRITION (PER SERVE)

CALS	FAT	SAT FAT	PROTEIN	CARBS
346	18.5g	15.9g	12g	29.7g

★★★★★ *I love this soup... it's simple and delicious and I love that it uses the entire broccoli.* **MANDYJANE13**

● EASY   ○ FAMILY-FRIENDLY   ● GLUTEN FREE   ● LOW CAL   ○ QUICK   ○ FREEZABLE

JAPANESE BEEF & NOODLE BROTH

Ready in 30 minutes, this quick and easy Asian noodle soup is nice and light while still satisfying the carnivore in you.

SERVES 4 **PREP** 15 mins **COOK** 15 mins

7cm-piece fresh ginger, peeled
1 tbs peanut oil
500g beef mince
2 garlic cloves, crushed
125ml (½ cup) mirin seasoning
1 tbs brown sugar
125ml (½ cup) light soy sauce
1.5L (6 cups) chicken stock
270g pkt soba noodles
3 baby buk choy, halved lengthways
50g snow peas, thinly sliced
    lengthways
2 green shallots, thinly sliced
    diagonally
2 soft-boiled eggs, peeled, halved
¼ tsp shichimi togarashi (see tip)

1 Finely grate 3cm ginger. Heat the oil in a large non-stick frying pan over high heat. Add the beef and cook, breaking up mince with a wooden spoon, for 4-5 minutes or until well browned. Add the garlic and grated ginger. Cook, stirring, for 1 minute or until aromatic. Add the mirin, sugar and half the soy sauce. Cook, stirring, over medium heat, for 2 minutes or liquid is reduced and mixture is sticky. Remove pan from heat.

2 Meanwhile, thinly slice the remaining ginger. Combine the stock, sliced ginger and remaining soy in a medium saucepan. Bring to the boil.

3 Cook the soba noodles following packet directions. Drain well.

4 Divide the noodles and buk choy among serving bowls. Ladle in the hot broth. Top with beef mixture, snow peas, shallot, egg and shichimi togarashi. Serve.

COOK'S TIP

Shichimi togarashi is a common Japanese hot spice mix containing seven ingredients, including chillies. You can buy it at supermarkets.

NUTRITION (PER SERVE)

CALS	FAT	SAT FAT	PROTEIN	CARBS
512	21.2g	8.8g	26.2g	47.6g

● EASY ○ FAMILY-FRIENDLY ○ GLUTEN FREE ○ LOW CAL ● QUICK ○ FREEZABLE

Very easy to make and very tasty. **AKUBRA17**

PORK & SWEET CORN
WONTON

There's no need to rush to the local Chinese takeaway joint for your next dumpling fix – this low-cal wonton soup is the business!

SERVES 4 **PREP** 35 mins **COOK** 15 mins

1L (4 cups) chicken stock
1 tbs light soy sauce
1 tbs Shaoxing wine (Chinese cooking wine)
3cm-piece fresh ginger, cut into matchsticks
1 long fresh red chilli, thinly sliced
1 cob sweetcorn, kernels removed
2 green shallots, thinly sliced diagonally
1 tsp sesame oil
½ cup fresh coriander leaves

WONTONS
300g pork mince
1 tbs fresh coriander, finely chopped
1 tbs hoisin sauce
1 green shallot, finely chopped
2 tsp fresh finely grated ginger
2 tsp light soy sauce
250g pkt wonton wrappers

1 To make the wontons, line a baking tray with baking paper. Combine the pork, coriander, hoisin, shallot, ginger and soy sauce in a bowl. Place a wonton wrapper on a flat work surface. Place 1 heaped tsp of pork mixture in the centre. Use a pastry brush dipped in water to brush edge of the wrapper, then fold wrapper over diagonally to enclose the filling. Brush 1 corner with water and fold around filling to meet the second corner. Press to secure. Place wonton on prepared tray. Repeat with remaining wrappers and filling.

2 Meanwhile, bring the stock, 500ml (2 cups) water, soy sauce, cooking wine, ginger and chilli to the boil in a saucepan over high heat. Reduce heat to medium. Add wontons and corn. Cook for 6 minutes or until wontons are cooked through. Stir in white section of shallot and the oil.

3 Ladle broth and wontons among serving bowls. Top with the coriander and green section of shallot, to serve.

COOK'S TIP

Save time by using bought pork wontons, or any other flavour you like. Simply omit step 1.

NUTRITION (PER SERVE)

CALS	FAT	SAT FAT	PROTEIN	CARBS
252	11g	3g	25g	45g

○ EASY ○ FAMILY-FRIENDLY ○ GLUTEN FREE ● LOW CAL ○ QUICK ○ FREEZABLE

★★★★★

This was relatively easy to make, and pretty tasty.
We will definitely make this again :) **TIGERLILLY20**

35
minutes
prep

UDON & PEKING DUCK BOWL

Asian flavours of Peking duck, udon noodles, buk choy and coriander are combined in this satisfying soup that's ready in a flash.

SERVES 4 **PREP** 10 mins **COOK** 15 mins

1 pkt (about 372g) ready-roasted peking duck breasts
1L (4 cups) chicken stock
4cm-piece fresh ginger, peeled, cut into matchsticks
2-3 tsp soy sauce, to taste
2 x 200g pkt fresh udon noodles
1 bunch baby buk choy, leaves and stems separated, sliced
100g oyster mushrooms, torn
⅓ cup fresh coriander leaves
2 green shallots, thinly sliced
1 long fresh red chilli, thinly sliced diagonally
1 tsp sesame oil

1 Preheat oven to 180°C/160°C fan forced. Line a baking tray with baking paper. Arrange duck on the prepared tray. Cook following packet directions. Rest for 5 minutes. Thinly slice.

2 Meanwhile, bring the stock, 250ml (1 cup) water, ginger and soy sauce to the boil over high heat. Add the noodles. Cook, stirring, for 1 minute. Add the buk choy stem and mushroom. Cook, stirring, for 1 minute or until stem is tender-crisp. Add buk choy leaves, half the coriander, half the shallot and half the chilli. Cook, stirring, for 1 minute or until leaves are just wilted and noodles are tender.

3 Ladle soup among serving bowls. Drizzle with oil. Top with duck, and the remaining coriander, shallot and chilli. Serve.

COOK'S TIP

If desired, swap the duck with 400g chicken thigh fillets marinated in a little soy and hoisin sauce. Pan-fry, turning, for 12 minutes or until cooked.

NUTRITION (PER SERVE)

CALS	FAT	SAT FAT	PROTEIN	CARBS
350	15g	4g	26g	27g

● EASY ○ FAMILY-FRIENDLY ○ GLUTEN FREE ● LOW CAL ● QUICK ○ FREEZABLE

Easy recipe. Great to impress guests with for a dinner party. I love it for a quick meal instead of takeaway. **DIDEDOC**

CHIANG MAI NOODLE

Enjoy a bowl of that unique Thai flavour balance of salty, sour and sweet in this quick chicken noodle soup that's sure to impress.

SERVES 4 **PREP** 10 mins **COOK** 20 mins

350g fresh chow mein egg noodles
400ml can coconut milk
2 tsp Thai red curry paste
¼ tsp ground turmeric
500ml (2 cups) chicken stock
500g chicken breast fillets, sliced
1 tbs brown sugar
1 tbs fish sauce
½ cup fresh basil leaves, plus
    extra, to serve

1 Cook the noodles in a saucepan of boiling salted water for 2 minutes or until just cooked. Drain. Refresh under cold running water. Drain well. Set aside.

2 Meanwhile, heat 125ml (½ cup) of the coconut milk in a wok over high heat. Cook, stirring, for 5 minutes or until the coconut milk splits. Add the curry paste and cook, stirring, for 1-2 minutes or until aromatic. Add the turmeric and stir to combine.

3 Add the stock and remaining coconut milk. Simmer for 5 minutes or until reduced slightly. Add the chicken and simmer for 5 minutes or until cooked through. Stir in the sugar, fish sauce and basil.

4 Divide noodles among serving bowls. Ladle over the soup. Sprinkle with extra basil leaves, season and serve.

COOK'S TIP

Add some greens with the chicken in step 3, if you like. Try broccoli florets and trimmed green beans.

NUTRITION (PER SERVE)

CALS	FAT	SAT FAT	PROTEIN	CARBS
601	24g	16g	41g	54g

★★★★★ *Good flavours and not too hot, but you could easily make it hotter by adding more curry paste.* **YOUCANCOOK**

● EASY ○ FAMILY-FRIENDLY ○ GLUTEN FREE ○ LOW CAL ● QUICK ○ FREEZABLE

JAPANESE CHICKEN & TOFU SOBA

You'll savour every spoonful of this miso-infused soup, especially the succulent poached chicken and golden roasted tofu croutons.

SERVES 4 **PREP** 35 mins **COOK** 25 mins

1L (4 cups) chicken stock
6cm-piece fresh ginger, peeled,
    cut into thin matchsticks
4 green shallots, sliced diagonally
    into 2cm lengths
2 (about 500g) chicken breasts
½ nori sheet, crumbled
125ml (½ cup) boiling water
250g firm tofu, cut into 1.5cm cubes
2 tsp sesame oil, plus an extra
    few drops
2 tsp soy sauce
180g soba noodles
115g (⅓ cup) white miso paste
125ml (½ cup) warm water
1 bunch gai lan, leaves cut into
    4cm pieces, stems separated
200g Swiss brown mushrooms, sliced
1 long fresh red chilli, thinly sliced
Toasted sesame seeds and
    lime wedges, to serve

1 Preheat oven to 200°C/180°C fan forced. Line a baking tray with baking paper.

2 Bring stock, ginger and half the shallot to the boil in a large saucepan over medium-high heat. Reduce heat to low. Add chicken. Poach for 15 minutes or until just cooked through. Transfer chicken to a board. Thinly slice diagonally.

3 Meanwhile, place nori in a heatproof bowl. Cover with boiling water. Set aside. Toss tofu, oil and soy in a bowl. Spread on prepared tray. Cook for 12 minutes or until golden.

4 Cook noodles in a saucepan of boiling water for 3 minutes or until just tender. Drain. Refresh under cold running water. Drain well. Toss with extra oil. Divide among serving bowls.

5 Combine miso and warm water in a jug. Drain nori liquid into soup, discarding nori. Bring soup to a simmer over low heat. Add gai lan stems and mushroom. Simmer for 2 minutes or until just tender. Add gai lan leaves, miso mixture and chicken. Stir for 1 minute or until warmed through.

6 Ladle soup among bowls. Top with tofu, chilli, remaining shallot and sesame seeds. Serve with lime wedges.

COOK'S TIP

To make this a vegan dish, simply omit the chicken and use vegetable stock.

NUTRITION (PER SERVE)

CALS	FAT	SAT FAT	PROTEIN	CARBS
411	11.5g	2.8g	39g	41.3g

○ EASY ○ FAMILY-FRIENDLY ○ GLUTEN FREE ● LOW CAL ○ QUICK ○ FREEZABLE

CHICKEN & VEGETABLE LAKSA

This creamy spicy soup may be very popular in South East Asia, but we're sure it will soon be in demand in your household, too.

SERVES 4 **PREP** 15 mins **COOK** 15 mins

250g pkt dried vermicelli noodles

1 tbs vegetable oil

185g jar Malaysian laksa paste

500ml (2 cups) salt-reduced chicken stock

2 x 270ml cans light coconut milk

2 tbs fish sauce

500g chicken breast fillets, thinly sliced

300g broccoli, cut into small florets

150g green beans, trimmed, cut into thirds

125g cherry tomatoes, halved

½ cup fresh mint leaves

130g (2 cups) bean sprouts, trimmed

40g (½ cup) fried shallots

Lime wedges, to serve

1 Place the noodles in a large heatproof bowl. Cover with boiling water. Stand for 5 minutes or until the noodles soften. Drain well.

2 Meanwhile, heat the oil in a wok over medium-high heat. Add the laksa paste. Cook, stirring, for 2-3 minutes or until aromatic. Add the stock, coconut milk and fish sauce. Bring to the boil. Add the chicken. Reduce the heat to medium-low and simmer for 5 minutes. Add the broccoli and beans. Simmer for 2 minutes. Add the tomato. Simmer for 1 minute or until broccoli is bright green and tender.

3 Divide noodles among serving bowls. Ladle laksa over the noodles. Top with mint, bean sprouts and fried shallots. Serve with lime wedges.

COOK'S TIP

For a prawn laksa, use 750g peeled green medium prawns instead of the chicken.

NUTRITION (PER SERVE)

CALS	FAT	SAT FAT	PROTEIN	CARBS
687	22.9g	8.9g	44g	71.5g

★★★★★ *Very simple to make and to create your own spin on it. We added extra vegies, but kept everything else as per recipe.* **ELLACHEF**

● EASY ○ FAMILY-FRIENDLY ○ GLUTEN FREE ○ LOW CAL ● QUICK ○ FREEZABLE

ITALIAN MEATBALL &
MACARONI

Using tasty Italian sausage to make cheat's meatballs, plus kid-friendly macaroni, this soup will get the thumbs up from the whole family.

SERVES 4 **PREP** 15 mins **COOK** 25 mins

375g extra-lean Italian-style
   sausages
1 tbs olive oil
1 red onion, chopped
1 red capsicum, chopped
1 tbs chicken stock powder
400g can chopped tomatoes
   with basil and garlic
80g (½ cup) dried macaroni pasta
300g broccoli, cut into small florets
1 tbs finely chopped fresh
   basil leaves
Finely grated parmesan, to serve

1 Squeeze the meat from the sausages. Roll 1 tsp of meat into a ball to make each meatball.

2 Heat the oil in a large saucepan over medium heat. Add the onion and capsicum. Cook, stirring, for 5 minutes or until the onion has softened. Stir in the stock powder, tomato and 1.25L (5 cups) water. Bring to the boil. Add the meatballs and pasta. Reduce the heat to medium-low. Simmer for 10 minutes.

3 Add the broccoli and simmer for 5 minutes or until the pasta is tender and the meatballs are cooked through. Stir in the basil. Serve soup topped with parmesan.

COOK'S TIP

Experiment with different flavoured sausages, if you like. Give bratwurst, chicken, Mexican or chorizo sausages a go.

NUTRITION (PER SERVE)

CALS	FAT	SAT FAT	PROTEIN	CARBS
323	12.7g	3.9g	21g	27.7g

★★★★★ *This was super easy to make. The kids even helped to roll the meatballs!* **MURRAY50**

● EASY ● FAMILY-FRIENDLY ○ GLUTEN FREE ● LOW CAL ○ QUICK ○ FREEZABLE

SLOW & HEARTY

SOUPS COOKED FOR AN HOUR OR MORE ENTICE WITH
A SMACK OF FLAVOUR. PREP, FORGET, SLURP, REPEAT.

SLOW-COOKED BEEF &
BARLEY

Slow-cooked soups can be healthy and low-cal, too, without scrimping on flavour. This one is crammed with nutritious cabbage and pearl barley.

SERVES 4   **PREP** 15 mins   **COOK** 8 hours 10 mins

2 tsp olive oil
500g beef blade steak, trimmed, chopped
2 carrots, peeled, finely chopped
2 celery sticks, trimmed, chopped
1 large brown onion, finely chopped
2 garlic cloves, crushed
2 tsp fresh thyme leaves
500ml (2 cups) beef stock
400g can diced tomatoes
75g (⅓ cup) pearl barley, rinsed, drained
120g cavolo nero (Tuscan cabbage), trimmed, coarsely chopped
2 tbs finely chopped fresh continental parsley
Baby continental parsley sprigs, to serve

1 Heat half the oil in a saucepan over high heat. Add the beef. Cook, stirring, for 2-3 minutes or until well browned. Transfer to a slow cooker.

2 Heat the remaining oil in the pan over medium heat. Add the carrot, celery and onion. Cook, stirring, for 5-6 minutes or until softened. Add the garlic and thyme. Cook, stirring, for 1 minute or until aromatic. Add to the slow cooker with the stock, 375ml (1½ cups) water and tomato. Cover and cook on Low for 6 hours.

3 Add the barley and cavolo nero. Cook for 2 hours or until the barley is tender and the cabbage is wilted.

4 Season with pepper. Stir through the chopped parsley. Serve scattered with parsley sprigs.

NUTRITION (PER SERVE)

CALS	FAT	SAT FAT	PROTEIN	CARBS
275	8g	2g	27g	21g

COOK'S TIP

Pearl barley is an ancient grain with plenty of health benefits. It is high in beta-glucan and is associated with reduced blood sugar levels and cholesterol. Plus, it may also aid weight loss and improve digestion.

● EASY   ● FAMILY-FRIENDLY   ○ GLUTEN FREE   ● LOW CAL   ○ QUICK   ○ FREEZABLE

★★★★★

A delicious soup; easy to make. **SHELLEY86**

15 *minutes prep*

PANCETTA & BORLOTTI

Cooked in the slow cooker, the borlotti beans become deliciously soft in our rich broth. They're also low-GI and are an excellent source of protein and fibre.

SERVES 4 **PREP** 15 mins (+ soaking) **COOK** 6 hours 10 mins

190g (1 cup) dried borlotti beans
1 tsp extra virgin olive oil
1 brown onion, finely chopped
4 celery sticks, finely chopped
1 large carrot, peeled,
   finely chopped
75g pancetta, finely chopped
3 garlic cloves, crushed
2 tsp finely chopped fresh
   rosemary leaves
1 long fresh red chilli, deseeded,
   finely chopped
500ml (2 cups) salt-reduced chicken
   or vegetable stock
120g cavolo nero (Tuscan cabbage),
   trimmed, coarsely chopped
4 slices rye bread, toasted
1½ tbs basil pesto
Fresh baby herbs, to serve (optional)

1 Place the borlotti beans in a bowl. Cover with water. Set aside for 8 hours or overnight to soak. Drain. Transfer to a saucepan. Cover with water. Bring to the boil over medium-high heat. Cook for 10 minutes. Drain well.

2 Heat the oil in a non-stick frying pan over medium heat. Add the onion, celery, carrot and pancetta. Cook, stirring, for 5 minutes or until vegies are softened. Add the garlic, rosemary and chilli. Cook, stirring, for 1 minute or until aromatic.

3 Place the onion mixture, drained beans, stock and 500ml (2 cups) water in a slow cooker. Cover and cook on Low for 6 hours, adding the cavolo nero in the last 15 minutes of cooking. Season with pepper.

4 Spread the toast with pesto. Ladle the soup among serving bowls. Top with the herbs, if using, and serve with pesto toast.

COOK'S TIP

It is very important to do the initial boil of the borlotti beans in order to eliminate naturally occurring properties in the beans that may be harmful.

NUTRITION (PER SERVE)

CALS	FAT	SAT FAT	PROTEIN	CARBS
368	9g	2g	20g	40g

★★★★★ *Very hearty dish for winter.* **GOTHEPS**

● EASY   ● FAMILY-FRIENDLY   ○ GLUTEN FREE   ● LOW CAL   ○ QUICK   ● FREEZABLE

15+
minutes
prep

SLOW-COOKED FREEKEH & LAMB

Freekeh is wheat that is picked while still green and so is higher in nutrients. It works well in this hearty soup, paired with lean lamb leg steaks.

SERVES 4 **PREP** 15 mins **COOK** 2 hours 30 mins

2 tsp extra virgin olive oil

400g lean lamb leg steaks, excess fat trimmed, cut into 1.5cm pieces

1 large brown onion, finely chopped

2 carrots, peeled, finely chopped

3 celery sticks, finely chopped

3 garlic cloves, thinly sliced

2 tsp finely grated lemon rind

1 tsp dried oregano leaves

500ml (2 cups) chicken stock

100g (½ cup) wholegrain freekeh, rinsed, drained (see tip)

200g green beans, sliced

150g (1 cup) frozen peas

90g (⅓ cup) natural yoghurt

2 tbs chopped fresh mint leaves, plus extra sprigs, to serve

1 Heat half the oil in a large saucepan over medium-high heat. Cook the lamb, in batches, turning, for 3-4 minutes or until browned. Transfer to a plate.

2 Reduce heat to medium. Heat the remaining oil in the pan. Add the onion, carrot and celery. Cook, stirring, for 5 minutes or until softened. Add the garlic, lemon rind and oregano. Cook, stirring, for 1 minute or until aromatic. Return lamb to the pan with the stock and 875ml (3½ cups) water. Bring to the boil. Add the freekeh. Reduce heat to low and simmer, covered, for 1½-2 hours or until lamb is tender.

3 Add the beans and peas to the lamb mixture. Simmer, uncovered, for 10 minutes or until vegetables are tender.

4 Meanwhile, combine the yoghurt and mint in a small bowl. Ladle soup among serving bowls. Dollop with mint yoghurt. Season and top with extra mint, to serve.

COOK'S TIP

If you can't find freekeh at the supermarket, try a health food shop or good green grocers. Replace with pearl barley, if you prefer.

NUTRITION (PER SERVE)

CALS	FAT	SAT FAT	PROTEIN	CARBS
339	8.6g	2.5g	28.2g	33g

★★★★★ *Sooooo good. The whole family loved this soup and have already demanded I make it again.* **HUSBO**

● EASY ● FAMILY-FRIENDLY ○ GLUTEN FREE ● LOW CAL ○ QUICK ● FREEZABLE

15
minutes
prep

TUSCAN BREAD SOUP

Also known as ribollita, meaning "reboiled", this soup is the king of cooking with leftovers. What veg and pantry staples do you need using up?

SERVES 4 **PREP** 20 mins **COOK** 1 hour

1 tbs extra virgin olive oil

500g root vegetables (such as carrot or potato), peeled, coarsely chopped

100g deli meat (such as pancetta, bacon, ham or prosciutto), coarsely chopped

1 tbs tomato paste

2 tomatoes, peeled, coarsely chopped

2 garlic cloves, crushed

¼-½ tsp dried chilli flakes, to taste

1.5L (6 cups) chicken or vegetable stock

1 fresh herb sprig (such as rosemary or thyme)

400g can beans (such as cannellini, borlotti or four bean mix), rinsed, drained

175g green vegetables (such as zucchini, broccoli, celery or green beans), chopped

100g chopped leafy greens (such as kale)

4 slices bread, toasted

1 Heat the oil in a large, heavy-based saucepan over medium heat. Add the root vegetables and deli meat. Cook, stirring often, for 5 minutes or until vegetables are softened. Add the tomato paste. Cook, stirring, for 1-2 minutes or until the paste darkens. Add tomato, garlic and chilli. Cook, stirring, for 2 minutes or until aromatic.

2 Add the stock and herbs. Increase heat to high and bring to the boil. Reduce the heat to low and simmer for 20 minutes. Add beans and green vegetables. Cook for 15 minutes or until the vegetables are tender. Stir in the leafy greens and cook for 3-4 minutes or until just wilted. Season.

3 Ladle the soup among serving bowls and serve with the toast for dunking.

COOK'S TIP

For a more traditional spin, tear the bread and add to soup in last 15 minutes of cooking.

NUTRITION (PER SERVE)

CALS	FAT	SAT FAT	PROTEIN	CARBS
384	11.4g	3g	20.7g	41.1g

● EASY ● FAMILY-FRIENDLY ○ GLUTEN FREE ● LOW CAL ○ QUICK ● FREEZABLE

SLOW-COOKER
MULLIGATAWNY

For a super-easy dinner, try this simple two-step curry chicken soup that's made in the slow cooker. No fuss, loads of flavour.

SERVES 4   **PREP** 10 mins   **COOK** 5 hours 30 mins

700g chicken thigh fillets,
    fat trimmed
1 tbs finely chopped fresh ginger
3 tsp ground cumin
2 tsp ground coriander
¼ tsp ground turmeric
1L (4 cups) chicken stock
250ml (1 cup) apple juice
110g (½ cup) yellow split peas
125ml (½ cup) passata
2 fresh bay leaves
1 small fresh curry leaf sprig
250g pkt microwave white rice
125ml (½ cup) coconut cream,
    plus extra, to serve
Chilli powder, to sprinkle

1 Place the chicken in a slow cooker. Sprinkle with ginger, cumin, coriander and turmeric. Season with pepper. Stir in the stock, apple juice, split peas, passata, and the bay and curry leaves. Cover and cook on High for 4 hours or until the split peas are tender.

2 Stir in the rice and coconut cream. Cook on High, covered, for 1½ hours or until the rice is tender. Ladle the soup among serving bowls. Drizzle over extra coconut cream and sprinkle with chilli powder, to serve.

NUTRITION (PER SERVE)

CALS	FAT	SAT FAT	PROTEIN	CARBS
354	13.2g	7.4g	24g	32.3g

COOK'S TIP

To freeze this soup, cool then place serving portions into airtight containers, allowing a 2cm gap at the top for expansion. Label and date. Freeze for up to 1 month.

★ ★ ★ ★ ★

Absolutely loved it. Nothing like throwing something in the slow cooker and not having to do anything else. **TLCO8O**

● EASY   ● FAMILY-FRIENDLY   ○ GLUTEN FREE   ● LOW CAL   ○ QUICK   ● FREEZABLE

INDIAN-SPICED LAMB &
CHICKPEA

Warm up your weeknights with this slow-cooker soup – it's packed with spices and tender lamb shanks, plus it's low-cal and gluten-free!

SERVES 4 **PREP** 15 mins **COOK** 7 hours

2 tsp extra virgin olive oil

2 (700g) French-trimmed lamb shanks

1 large brown onion, finely chopped

1 carrot, peeled, finely chopped

2 celery sticks, finely chopped

2 garlic cloves, crushed

2 tsp cumin seeds, crushed

2 tsp brown mustard seeds

2 tsp sweet paprika

1 tsp ground coriander

400g can diced tomatoes

400g can chickpeas, rinsed, drained

500ml (2 cups) gluten-free chicken stock

100g trimmed silverbeet (about ½ bunch), chopped

Natural yoghurt, to serve (optional)

1 Heat half the oil in a large non-stick frying pan over high heat. Add the lamb and cook for 1-2 minutes each side or until browned. Transfer to a slow cooker.

2 Heat remaining oil in the pan over medium heat. Add the onion, carrot and celery. Cook, stirring, for 5 minutes or until softened. Add the garlic, cumin, mustard, paprika and coriander. Cook, stirring, for 1 minute. Transfer to the slow cooker. Stir in tomato, chickpeas, stock and 500ml (2 cups) water. Cover. Cook on Low for 6 hours 30 minutes.

3 Transfer lamb to a bowl. When cool enough to handle, use 2 forks to shred meat, discarding bones. Return the meat to the slow cooker. Add the silverbeet and cook for 20 minutes. Season. Serve with yoghurt, if using.

COOK'S TIP

The flavour of this soup will intensify upon resting. Any leftovers can be placed in an airtight container and kept in the fridge for up to 3 days.

NUTRITION (PER SERVE)

CALS	FAT	SAT FAT	PROTEIN	CARBS
269	11g	3g	24g	16g

★★★★★ *Whole family loved this; the smell while it was cooking was amazing. Will definitely make again.* **MELK83**

● EASY ● FAMILY-FRIENDLY ● GLUTEN FREE ● LOW CAL ○ QUICK ● FREEZABLE

FIVE-A-DAY
MINESTRONE

For a healthy soup, try our veg-packed minestrone with power pesto.
Ready in just over an hour it will fill you up and keep you going.

SERVES 6 **PREP** 25 mins **COOK** 40 mins

1 tbs olive oil, plus extra, to drizzle
150g pancetta slices, chopped
¼ tsp fennel seeds (optional)
1 large brown onion, finely chopped
2 large carrots, peeled,
　finely chopped
2 celery sticks, finely chopped
1 red capsicum, finely chopped
3 garlic cloves, crushed
700g btl passata
500ml (2 cups) beef stock
400g can borlotti beans,
　rinsed, drained
400g can chickpeas, rinsed, drained
50g (¼ cup) dried risoni pasta
2 zucchini, finely chopped
½ cup chopped purple kale,
　plus extra leaves, to serve

PESTO
75g broccoli florets
60g baby spinach
1 cup fresh basil leaves, plus
　extra leaves, to serve
25g (⅓ cup) shredded parmesan
1 small garlic clove, chopped
1 lemon, rind finely grated, juiced
2 tbs olive oil

1 Heat the oil in a large saucepan over medium heat. Add the pancetta and cook, stirring, for 2 minutes or until just golden. Stir in fennel, if using, until aromatic. Add the onion, carrot, celery, capsicum and garlic. Cook, stirring, for 10 minutes or until vegies are softened.

2 Add the passata, stock and 250ml (1 cup) water. Bring to the boil. Reduce heat to low. Cover and simmer for 5 minutes. Add the beans and chickpeas. Cover and simmer for 5 minutes or until thickened slightly. Add the pasta. Simmer, partially covered, stirring occasionally, for 10 minutes or until pasta is al dente. Add the zucchini and kale. Simmer, partially covered, for 3 minutes or until zucchini is just tender. Season with pepper.

3 Meanwhile, to make the pesto, microwave the broccoli in a microwave-safe bowl for 1 minute or until tender. Cool slightly. Place in a food processor with the spinach, basil, parmesan, garlic and lemon rind. Process until finely chopped. With motor running, add the lemon juice and oil, and process until smooth.

4 Season soup. Ladle among serving bowls. Top with pesto and the extra basil and kale. Drizzle with extra oil. Serve.

COOK'S TIP

Do you have a fridge crisper filled with vegies that need using up? You can easily swap out any veg in this soup with the equivalent amount of another veg. Go for it!

NUTRITION (PER SERVE)

CALS	FAT	SAT FAT	PROTEIN	CARBS
403	19.5g	4.5g	20.5g	30.5g

● EASY　● FAMILY-FRIENDLY　○ GLUTEN FREE　● LOW CAL　○ QUICK　● FREEZABLE

BEEF STROGANOFF SOUP

People have loved beef stroganoff for decades, and now you can enjoy it as a soup! This version is just as rich and creamy as you would expect.

SERVES 6 **PREP** 15 mins **COOK** 2 hours 5 mins

750ml (3 cups) chicken stock
10g dried whole porcini mushrooms
700g piece beef topside roast
   (see tips)
80ml (⅓ cup) extra virgin olive oil
2 brown onions, thinly sliced
3 sprigs fresh thyme
1 dried bay leaf
3 garlic cloves, finely chopped
250g button mushrooms,
   thickly sliced
250g fusilli avellinesi pasta (see tips)
125ml (½ cup) thickened cream
Coarsely chopped fresh chives,
   to serve

1 Bring the stock and 750ml (3 cups) water to the boil in a saucepan over high heat. Add porcini. Set aside.

2 Meanwhile, season beef. Heat 1 tbs oil in a large saucepan over high heat. Add beef. Cook, turning, for 8 minutes or until well browned. Transfer to a plate. Wipe pan clean.

3 Heat 2 tbs remaining oil in the pan over high heat. Add the onion, thyme and bay leaf. Season. Cook, stirring occasionally, for 6 minutes or until onion is softened. Reduce heat to medium. Add the garlic and cook, stirring, for 4 minutes or until the onion is well browned.

4 Strain stock mixture into onion mixture. Coarsely chop porcini and add to pan. Add beef. Bring to the boil. Cover. Reduce heat to medium-low. Cook for 1½ hours or until beef is tender.

5 Meanwhile, heat the remaining oil in a large frying pan over high heat. Add button mushroom. Cook, stirring occasionally, for 5 minutes or until golden.

6 Transfer beef to a clean board. Use 2 forks to shred meat. Remove and discard herbs. Return beef to pan. Bring to the boil. Add fried mushroom and pasta. Simmer, partially covered, for 15 minutes or until pasta is just tender. Stir in cream. Serve soup sprinkled with chives.

COOK'S TIPS

You can use any short pasta for this recipe. So that the beef cooks evenly, make sure it is immersed in the stock mixture. If the roast is too big, cut it in half.

NUTRITION (PER SERVE)

CALS	FAT	SAT FAT	PROTEIN	CARBS
536	26.8g	9.2g	37.8g	34.2g

● EASY   ● FAMILY-FRIENDLY   ○ GLUTEN FREE   ○ LOW CAL   ○ QUICK   ○ FREEZABLE

CHILLI & BLACK BEAN PULLED PORK

If you love pulled pork, wait until you try it in this soup! With tomatoes, pumpkin and spices, it will smell incredible as it cooks.

SERVES 6 **PREP** 30 mins **COOK** 8 hours 15 mins

1½ tbs extra virgin olive oil

1kg boneless pork shoulder, rind removed, trimmed

1 large red capsicum

2 brown onions, finely chopped

4 garlic cloves, crushed

1 tbs dried oregano leaves

2 tsp ground cumin

1 tsp ground coriander

1½ tsp smoked paprika

½-1 tsp chilli flakes, to taste

1 tbs tomato paste

400g can chopped tomatoes

1L (4 cups) gluten-free chicken stock

400g can black beans, rinsed, drained

3 large (about 500g) zucchini, cut into 5cm pieces

600g butternut pumpkin, peeled, cut into 3cm pieces

Corn tortilla strips, sour cream, chopped avocado, fresh coriander leaves and lime wedges, to serve

1 Heat 2 tsp oil in the flameproof bowl of a slow cooker (see tip). Add the pork. Cook, turning, for 4-6 minutes or until browned. Transfer to a plate and set aside.

2 Finely chop half the capsicum. Slice remaining capsicum into strips and reserve. Add onion to the slow cooker. Cook, stirring, for 3 minutes or until softened. Add chopped capsicum. Cook, stirring, for 2 minutes or until just softened. Add the garlic, oregano, cumin, coriander, paprika and chilli, to taste. Cook, stirring, for 1 minute or until aromatic. Stir in the tomato paste. Stir in the tomato.

3 Return pork to the slow cooker. Stir in the stock. Cover. Cook on Low for 6 hours. Add beans, zucchini, pumpkin and reserved sliced capsicum. Cook, covered, on Low for 2 hours or until the meat and vegetables are tender.

4 Transfer pork to a clean board and use 2 forks to coarsely shred. Return to the slow cooker. Gently stir to combine, taking care not to break up the vegies. Season.

5 Ladle the soup among serving bowls. Top with the tortilla strips, sour cream, avocado and coriander. Serve with the lime wedges.

COOK'S TIP

If your slow cooker doesn't have a flameproof bowl, simply complete steps 1 and 2 using a large non-stick frying pan, then transfer the mixture to the slow cooker.

NUTRITION (PER SERVE)

CALS	FAT	SAT FAT	PROTEIN	CARBS
622	31g	11g	37g	42g

● EASY ● FAMILY-FRIENDLY ● GLUTEN FREE ○ LOW CAL ○ QUICK ○ FREEZABLE

GREEK LEMON
CHICKEN

Known as avgolemono, this creamy Greek soup cooks in the slow cooker until the chicken and rice are gorgeously tender. Yum!

SERVES 4 **PREP** 10 mins **COOK** 6 hours 5 mins

600g chicken breast fillets

1.25L (5 cups) gluten-free
  chicken stock

2 dried bay leaves

2 garlic cloves, crushed

150g (⅔ cup) medium-grain
  white rice

2 eggs, at room temperature
  (see tip)

60ml (¼ cup) fresh lemon juice

80g marinated feta in oil,
  drained, crumbled

¼ cup chopped fresh continental
  parsley leaves

Finely grated lemon rind, to serve

1 Place the chicken, stock, 875ml (3½ cups) water, bay leaves, garlic and rice in a slow cooker. Cover. Cook on Low for 6 hours (or High for 3 hours) or until chicken is tender.

2 Use tongs to transfer the chicken to a heatproof bowl. Using 2 forks, shred chicken. Remove and discard the bay leaves.

3 Whisk the eggs and lemon juice in a bowl. Gradually add 125ml (½ cup) of the hot stock mixture, whisking until combined. Return three-quarters of the chicken meat to the soup. Stir in egg mixture. Cook, stirring, on High for 5 minutes or until soup whitens and thickens slightly. Season.

4 Ladle soup among serving bowls. Top with the remaining chicken, feta, parsley and lemon rind. Serve.

COOK'S TIP

Make sure your eggs are at room temperature before mixing with the lemon juice and adding the hot stock. This will help to incorporate the eggs properly.

NUTRITION (PER SERVE)

CALS	FAT	SAT FAT	PROTEIN	CARBS
413	11.2g	5.4g	44.1g	32.1g

★★★★★ *Where has this been my whole life? So delicious, so creamy, so easy to make with common ingredients. It's basically soupy risotto with lemon sauce.* **TASWEGIA_TWC**

● EASY ● FAMILY-FRIENDLY ● GLUTEN FREE ● LOW CAL ○ QUICK ○ FREEZABLE

SWEET POTATO & CHICKPEA

Flavoured with Moroccan spices, including cumin, harissa, paprika and garlic, this soup is easy for your slow cooker to manage – all you have to do is wait!

SERVES 4 **PREP** 20 mins **COOK** 8 hours 10 mins

1 tbs extra virgin olive oil

1 tsp ground cumin

2 brown onions, finely chopped

3 large garlic cloves, crushed

285g jar roasted red peppers, drained, rinsed, halved

2 tsp gluten-free harissa paste

2 large (about 800g) sweet potatoes, peeled, cut into 5cm pieces

3 large carrots, peeled, chopped

1L (4 cups) gluten-free vegetable stock

400g can chickpeas, rinsed, drained

1 tsp honey

1 tsp turmeric

Greek yoghurt, to serve

Baby coriander leaves, to serve (optional)

SPICED CHICKPEAS

2 tsp extra virgin olive oil

400g can chickpeas, rinsed, drained, patted dry

2 tbs pepitas

½ tsp ground cumin

½ tsp smoked paprika

1 Heat the oil in a large frying pan over medium heat. Add the cumin and cook, stirring, for 30 seconds or until aromatic. Add the onion. Cook, stirring, for 3-4 minutes or until softened. Add the garlic, peppers and harissa. Cook, stirring, for 2 minutes or until aromatic. Transfer to a slow cooker. Wipe pan clean with paper towel.

2 Add the sweet potato, carrot, stock, chickpeas, honey and turmeric to the slow cooker. Season with pepper. Stir to combine. Cover. Cook on Low for 6-8 hours or until vegetables are tender.

3 Use a stick blender to blend soup in slow cooker until smooth. Stir in up to 250ml (1 cup) water if the soup is too thick. Season.

4 Meanwhile, to make the spiced chickpeas, heat the oil in the frying pan over medium-high heat. Add the chickpeas, pepitas, cumin and paprika. Cook, shaking pan occasionally, for 6-10 minutes or until crisp. Season.

5 Ladle soup among serving bowls. Top with yoghurt and the chickpea mixture. Sprinkle with coriander, if using. Season and serve.

COOK'S TIP

Harissa is a Northern African chilli paste, made with chillies, garlic and spices, such as coriander, paprika and cumin. If you're not a fan of a lot of spice, halve the amount in the recipe. Also, if gluten intolerant, check the label, as some brands contain gluten.

NUTRITION (PER SERVE)

CALS	FAT	SAT FAT	PROTEIN	CARBS
317	10g	2g	9g	41g

● EASY ● FAMILY-FRIENDLY ● GLUTEN FREE ● LOW CAL ○ QUICK ● FREEZABLE

CURRIED CHICKPEA & LAMB

You know those spices lurking in the pantry? Put them to good use in this wonderful belly-warming soup with pappadums for dunking.

SERVES 6 **PREP** 20 mins **COOK** 7 hours 45 mins

1 tbs olive oil

4 French-trimmed lamb shanks

1 large brown onion,
   sliced into rings

2 garlic cloves, crushed

2 tsp finely grated fresh ginger

1 tsp ground turmeric

1 tsp ground coriander

¼ tsp ground cinnamon

¼ tsp cayenne pepper

Pinch of ground cloves

200g (1 cup) dried chickpeas,
   rinsed, drained

2L (8 cups) chicken stock

270ml can coconut cream

350g sweet potato, peeled,
   cut into 1.5cm pieces

120g baby spinach

Tzatziki, micro herbs (optional)
   and pappadams, to serve

1 Heat the oil in the flameproof bowl of a slow cooker. Add the lamb shanks and cook, turning often, for 8 minutes or until golden. Transfer to a plate.

2 Add onion to the bowl and reduce heat to medium. Cook, stirring, for 5 minutes or until softened and lightly golden. Add the garlic, ginger, turmeric, coriander, cinnamon, cayenne pepper and cloves. Cook, stirring, for 1 minute or until aromatic. Stir in the chickpeas, stock and coconut cream. Return lamb to the slow cooker and stir to coat. Cover and cook on Low for 6 hours.

3 Add sweet potato. Cook on Low for 1 hour 30 minutes or until the sweet potato is tender. Use a slotted spoon to transfer lamb to a large plate. Cool slightly. Use 2 forks to shred the meat, discarding the fat, sinew and bones.

4 Stir spinach into soup. Cover and set aside until spinach wilts. Return lamb to the soup and stir to combine. Ladle soup among serving bowls. Season. Top with the tzatziki and micro herbs, if using. Serve with the pappadums.

COOK'S TIP

Don't have a slow cooker with a flameproof bowl? Brown the lamb, onion and spices in a large deep frying pan over medium-high heat, then transfer to the slow cooker.

NUTRITION (PER SERVE)

CALS	FAT	SAT FAT	PROTEIN	CARBS
497	24g	13g	34g	34g

○ EASY ● **FAMILY-FRIENDLY** ○ GLUTEN FREE ○ LOW CAL ○ QUICK ○ FREEZABLE

FULLY LOADED
PEA SOUP

Topped with maple bacon and cheesy toast, enjoy a creamy slow-cooker soup that is chock-full of peas and will hit the hot spot every time.

SERVES 6 **PREP** 10 mins **COOK** 8 hours 15 mins

500g bacon bones
500g green split peas
2L (8 cups) salt-reduced
   chicken stock
450g (3 cups) frozen peas
Sour cream and sliced green
   shallots, to serve

TOPPING
8 rashers (about 200g)
   streaky bacon
1 tbs maple syrup
4 thick slices sourdough
100g (1 cup) pre-grated 4-cheese
   blend or mozzarella

1 Place the bacon bones, split peas and stock in a slow cooker. Cover and cook on High for 6-8 hours or until soup is very thick.

2 Remove the bacon bones from the soup and discard. Add the frozen peas and stand for 5 minutes to heat through. Use a stick blender to blend soup in the slow cooker until smooth.

3 To make the topping, preheat oven to 200°C/180°C fan forced. Line a large baking tray with baking paper or foil. Arrange the bacon on the tray in a single layer. Brush with half the maple syrup. Bake for 4 minutes. Turn over and brush with the remaining maple syrup. Cook for a further 4 minutes or until golden. Transfer to a plate and set aside to cool (bacon will crisp up on cooling). Arrange bread on the tray. Cook for 2 minutes or until toasted. Turn over and top with cheese. Bake for 3 minutes or until cheese is melted.

4 Ladle soup among serving bowls. Top with the cheesy croutons, sour cream, maple bacon and shallot. Serve.

COOK'S TIP

Leftover soup may thicken further when kept in the fridge. You can thin with stock or water until you reach your desired consistency.

NUTRITION (PER SERVE)

CALS	FAT	SAT FAT	PROTEIN	CARBS
654	22.5	11.5g	36.7g	67.9g

● EASY ● FAMILY-FRIENDLY ○ GLUTEN FREE ○ LOW CAL ○ QUICK ● FREEZABLE

SLOW-COOKER CHICKEN NOODLE

Slowly does it for an easy chicken and veg-packed soup with hungry-busting linguine noodles. You'll taste the goodness in every slurp.

SERVES 4 **PREP** 15 mins **COOK** 3 hours 30 mins

2 small chicken breast fillets
2 carrots, peeled, chopped
2 celery stalks, chopped
1 brown onion, chopped
2 garlic cloves, crushed
4 fresh thyme sprigs
4 fresh continental parsley sprigs,
    plus extra ¼ cup coarsely
    chopped parsley leaves
2 dried bay leaves
1.5L (6 cups) chicken stock
150g dried linguine

1 Place the chicken, carrot, celery, onion, garlic, thyme and parsley sprigs, bay leaves, stock and 500ml (2 cups) water in a slow cooker. Cover. Cook on High for 3 hours (or Low for 6 hours) or until chicken is tender and just cooked through.

2 Remove and discard thyme, parsley and bay leaves. Transfer chicken to a clean board. Using 2 forks, shred chicken. Return chicken to slow cooker with the linguine. Season well. Cook on High for 30 minutes or until pasta is al dente. Stir in half the chopped parsley.

3 Ladle soup among serving bowls. Serve topped with remaining chopped parsley.

COOK'S TIP

Try leaving the skin on the carrots for added nutrients such as vitamin C, beta-carotene, and niacin.

NUTRITION (PER SERVE)

CALS	FAT	SAT FAT	PROTEIN	CARBS
316	2.8g	0.8g	32.5g	37.3g

★★★★★

This really is chicken soup for the soul. Loved it! **SHAWNSALAD**

● EASY   ● FAMILY-FRIENDLY   ○ GLUTEN FREE   ● LOW CAL   ○ QUICK   ○ FREEZABLE

MEGA-VEG
MINESTRONE

With six vegies per serve, your family will absorb the goodness in every spoonful. Why not slow cook a double batch for work lunches?

SERVES 4   **PREP** 25 mins   **COOK** 3 hours 30 mins

1 brown onion, chopped
2 carrots, finely chopped
2 celery stalks, finely chopped
1 large zucchini, finely chopped
1 swede, peeled, finely chopped
3 middle bacon rashers, trimmed, chopped
2 x 400g cans crushed tomatoes
1L (4 cups) chicken stock
2 tsp chopped fresh rosemary leaves
2 dried bay leaves
2 garlic cloves, crushed
420g can cannellini beans, rinsed, drained
80g (½ cup) dried macaroni
¼ cup coarsely chopped fresh basil leaves, plus extra leaves, to serve
Grated parmesan and crusty bread, to serve

1 Place the onion, carrot, celery, zucchini, swede, bacon, tomato, stock, 500ml (2 cups) water, rosemary, bay leaves and garlic in a slow cooker. Season. Cover. Cook on High for 3 hours (or Low for 6 hours).

2 Remove and the discard bay leaves. Add the beans and macaroni to the slow cooker. Cook on High for 30 minutes or until the macaroni is tender. Stir in the basil.

3 Top the soup with extra basil. Season. Serve with parmesan, for sprinkling, and the crusty bread.

NUTRITION (PER SERVE)

CALS	FAT	SAT FAT	PROTEIN	CARBS
501	12.7g	5.2g	26.8g	61g

COOK'S TIP

This soup is a great excuse to use up any excess veg you may have, so feel free to swap out any vegies in the recipe for the equivalent amount of another veg.

★★★★★

Very hearty soup. Changed the swede for parsnip. **DAISYDAISY11**

● EASY   ● FAMILY-FRIENDLY   ○ GLUTEN FREE   ○ LOW CAL   ○ QUICK   ○ FREEZABLE

25
minutes
prep

HEARTY BEEF
BORSCHT

Beef up your menu and get stuck into this hearty beetroot soup that will boost your intake of fibre, folate, manganese, potassium, iron and vitamin C.

SERVES 4 **PREP** 20 mins (+ cooling) **COOK** 1 hour 15 mins

2 tbs extra virgin olive oil, plus extra, to serve (optional)

400g beef chuck steak, trimmed, cut into 5cm pieces

1 brown onion, finely chopped

1 garlic clove, crushed

600g beetroot, peeled, coarsely chopped (see tip)

2 large cream delight potatoes, peeled, coarsely chopped

1 carrot, coarsely chopped

1 celery stalk, coarsely chopped

500ml (2 cups) gluten-free beef stock

2 tbs red wine vinegar

1 dried bay leaf

60ml (¼ cup) sour cream

2 tbs fresh dill sprigs

1 Heat half the oil in a large saucepan over medium heat. Add beef. Cook, stirring, for 5 minutes or until browned. Transfer to a bowl. Heat remaining oil in pan. Add the onion and garlic. Cook, stirring, for 5 minutes or until softened.

2 Return beef to pan with beetroot, potato, carrot, celery, stock, vinegar, bay leaf and 500ml (2 cups) water. Bring to the boil. Reduce heat to low. Simmer, covered, for 1 hour or until beef is tender. Discard bay leaf. Cool for 10 minutes.

3 Using a slotted spoon, transfer beef to a clean board. Using 2 forks, shred beef.

4 Using a stick blender, blend soup in pan until smooth. Return half of the beef to the soup. Season. Ladle the soup among serving bowls. Top with sour cream and the remaining beef. Drizzle with extra oil, if using. Season and sprinkle with dill, to serve.

COOK'S TIP

You will need about 3 medium beetroot for this recipe. Wear gloves when peeling and chopping to prevent your hands from staining.

NUTRITION (PER SERVE)

CALS	FAT	SAT FAT	PROTEIN	CARBS
429	22g	7.8g	272g	24.9g

★★★★★ *This version of borscht is a great way to get the kids to eat lots of vegies. Thank you.* **SHAWNSALAD**

● EASY ● FAMILY-FRIENDLY ● GLUTEN FREE ● LOW CAL ○ QUICK ● FREEZABLE

SLOW LAMB & BARLEY

This healthy slow cooker soup is a great dinner to add to the weekly rotation. Meat, vegies and earthy barley make a nourishing flavour combo.

SERVES 4 **PREP** 20 mins **COOK** 4 hours 5 mins

1 tbs extra virgin olive oil
2 (500g) lamb shanks
1 large leek, trimmed, chopped
2 carrots, chopped
2 large celery stalks, chopped
1 swede, peeled, chopped
2 garlic cloves, thinly sliced
1.5L (6 cups) chicken stock
110g (½ cup) pearl barley, rinsed
80g (½ cup) frozen peas
¼ cup chopped fresh continental parsley leaves, plus extra sprigs, to serve
Crusty bread, to serve

1 Heat the oil in the flameproof bowl of a slow cooker. Cook lamb, turning, for 5 minutes or until browned.

2 Add the leek, carrot, celery, swede, garlic, stock and 500ml (2 cups) water. Season. Cover. Cook on High for 4 hours (or Low for 8 hours), adding barley for the last 1½ hours of cooking.

3 Add peas to the slow cooker. Remove lamb from soup and place on a clean board. Use 2 forks to shred meat, discarding bones. Return lamb to soup. Stir in the parsley. Ladle among serving bowls. Top with parsley sprigs. Serve with the bread.

COOK'S TIP

If your slow cooker doesn't have a flameproof insert, brown the lamb in a frying pan, before placing in the slow cooker.

NUTRITION (PER SERVE)

CALS	FAT	SAT FAT	PROTEIN	CARBS
632	29.2g	10.1g	32.3g	54.9g

★★★★★

We loved the chunky vegetables and pearl barley in this soup. With the beef it was a real meal in a bowl. **CHACHA**

● EASY ● FAMILY-FRIENDLY ○ GLUTEN FREE ○ LOW CAL ○ QUICK ● FREEZABLE

20 minutes prep

HEARTY GREEK
MOUSSAKA

We transformed the hugely popular Greek dish into a generous eggplant soup bursting with flavour and 3.5 vegies per serve.

SERVES 6 **PREP** 20 mins **COOK** 2 hours 20 mins

2 lamb shanks
80ml (⅓ cup) extra virgin olive oil
1 brown onion, finely chopped
3 garlic cloves, thinly sliced
1 dried bay leaf
2 tbs tomato paste
½ tsp ground allspice
½ tsp ground cinnamon
400g can diced tomatoes
500ml (2 cups) chicken stock
400g can chickpeas, rinsed, drained
1 tsp dried oregano
2 eggplants, partially peeled
   (optional, see tip), cut into
   1.5cm pieces
Plain low-fat Greek-style yoghurt,
   shredded fresh mint leaves
   and chargrilled Lebanese
   bread, to serve

1 Season lamb. Heat 1 tbs oil in a large saucepan over high heat. Add lamb. Cook, turning, for 8 minutes or until browned all over. Transfer to a plate.

2 Reduce the heat to medium. Add the onion, garlic and bay leaf. Cook, stirring occasionally, for 5 minutes or until onion is softened. Add the tomato paste and spices. Cook, stirring, for 1 minute or until aromatic. Add tomato, stock, chickpeas, oregano and 500ml (2 cups) water. Bring to the boil. Cover. Reduce heat to medium-low. Cook for 1 hour 40 minutes or until lamb is very tender.

3 Meanwhile, heat 1½ tbs remaining oil in a large frying pan over high heat. Add half the eggplant. Cook, stirring occasionally, for 10 minutes or until golden. Transfer to a plate. Repeat with remaining oil and eggplant.

4 Remove and discard bay leaf. Using tongs, transfer lamb to a clean board. Use 2 forks to shred meat, discarding bones. Return to pan with the eggplant. Simmer, covered, for 20 minutes. Ladle soup among serving bowls. Dollop with yoghurt. Sprinkle with mint. Season. Serve with bread.

COOK'S TIP

To partially peel an eggplant, use a vegie peeler to peel off 1 strip lengthways. Leave a strip of skin, then peel another strip. Work your way around the eggplant to create stripes.

NUTRITION (PER SERVE)

CALS	FAT	SAT FAT	PROTEIN	CARBS
463	22.5g	6g	22.6g	38.3g

● EASY ● FAMILY-FRIENDLY ○ GLUTEN FREE ○ LOW CAL ○ QUICK ● FREEZABLE

MEXICAN CHICKEN &
CORN

Cooked in the slow cooker, the family can now enjoy Mexican in soup form!
Use the corn chips to scoop up a satisfying mouthful, or more.

SERVES 4 **PREP** 20 mins **COOK** 6 hours 45 minutes

2 tsp olive oil
4 chicken thigh fillets, fat trimmed
1 brown onion, finely chopped
2 garlic cloves, crushed
1.5L (6 cups) gluten-free
   chicken stock
3 tsp chipotle in adobo sauce
4 corncobs, husks and silk removed
400g can black beans, rinsed,
   drained
2 tbs fresh lime juice
85g (⅓ cup) sour cream
Hot chilli sauce, to drizzle
2 green shallots, thinly sliced
¼ cup fresh coriander sprigs
Lime cheeks and blue
   corn chips (see tip), to serve

1 Heat the oil in a large frying pan over medium heat.
Add the chicken. Cook for 3 minutes on each side or
until golden. Transfer to a slow cooker. Add the onion to the
frying pan and cook, stirring, for 5 minutes or until softened
and lightly golden. Add the garlic and cook, stirring, for
30 seconds or until aromatic. Transfer to the slow cooker.

2 Add stock to the slow cooker. Stir in the chipotle and
corncobs. Cover and cook on Low for 6 hours.

3 Use tongs to transfer the corncobs and chicken to
a chopping board. Cool slightly. Use a small sharp
knife to cut the corn kernels from the cobs. Coarsely chop
the chicken. Return corn and chicken meat to the slow
cooker. Add the beans and stir to combine. Cover and
cook on High for 30 minutes.

4 Stir the lime juice into the soup. Ladle soup among
serving bowls. Top with sour cream, chilli sauce, shallot
and coriander. Serve with lime cheeks and corn chips.

NUTRITION (PER SERVE)

CALS	FAT	SAT FAT	PROTEIN	CARBS
609	26g	10g	42g	43g

● EASY ● FAMILY-FRIENDLY ● GLUTEN FREE ○ LOW CAL ○ QUICK ○ FREEZABLE

★★★★★

We all love Mexican and this was fun to make and eat. **MS50**

CREAMY BROCCOLI & 3-CHEESE

For an easy no-fuss midweek meal, dig your spoons into this deliciously thick vegetarian soup made in the slow cooker. There's only 10 minutes prep time!

SERVES 6 **PREP** 10 mins **COOK** 6 hours 5 mins

1.2kg broccoli, stems trimmed
   (see tip)
400g cream delight potatoes, peeled
505g can potato and leek soup
4 garlic cloves, peeled
1L (4 cups) gluten-free
   plant-based chicken stock
190g (1¼ cups) frozen peas
125g cream cheese, chopped,
   softened
80g (1 cup) grated cheddar
2 tbs finely chopped fresh chives
40g (½ cup) finely grated parmesan,
   plus extra, to serve
Extra virgin olive oil, to serve

1 Place the broccoli, potato, soup, garlic, stock and 250ml (1 cup) water in a slow cooker. Cover. Cook on Low for 6 hours (or High for 3 hours) or until the vegetables are tender. Add the peas. Cook, covered, for 5 minutes.

2 Use a stick blender to blend soup in the slow cooker until smooth. Add the cheeses. Stir until melted and smooth. Season.

3 Ladle the soup among serving bowls. Top with the chives, extra parmesan and a drizzle of oil. Season with pepper and serve.

COOK'S TIP

You only need to trim about 1cm off the broccoli stems. Also, there is no need to cut the broccoli into small florets, simply place the whole heads in the slow cooker.

NUTRITION (PER SERVE)

CALS	FAT	SAT FAT	PROTEIN	CARBS
382	19.2g	11.2g	24.9g	20.5g

★★★★★

Even my fussy husband came back for a second bowl – delicious! **EHARRIO5**

● EASY ● FAMILY-FRIENDLY ○ GLUTEN FREE ● LOW CAL ○ QUICK ● FREEZABLE

MEXICAN MIXED BEAN AMIGO

With just 10 minutes of prep to do, you'll have plenty of time to hang with your fondest amigos before sharing in this spicy bowl.

SERVES 4 **PREP** 10 mins **COOK** 6 hours 5 mins

1 red capsicum, coarsely chopped
300g jar chunky chipotle salsa
30g pkt salt-reduced taco spice mix
400g can diced tomatoes
2 corncobs, husks and silk removed
3 tsp vegetable stock powder
400g can red kidney beans,
    rinsed, drained
1 tbs brown sugar
400g can black beans, rinsed, drained
¼ cup chopped fresh coriander
    leaves, plus extra sprigs, to serve
85g (⅓ cup) sour cream
Sliced fresh green chilli, lime wedges
    and chargrilled tortillas, to serve

1 Place the capsicum, salsa, spice mix, tomato, corn, stock powder, kidney beans, sugar and 1L (4 cups) water in a slow cooker. Cover. Cook on Low for 6 hours (or High for 3 hours) or until thickened slightly.

2 Use tongs to transfer corncobs to a chopping board. Stir the black beans and coriander into the slow cooker. Cook, covered, on High for 5 minutes. Season.

3 Meanwhile, using a sharp knife, remove kernels from the cobs in large chunks. Stir into to the soup.

4 Ladle soup among serving bowls. Top with sour cream. Sprinkle with chilli and extra coriander. Serve with the lime wedges and tortillas.

NUTRITION (PER SERVE)

CALS	FAT	SAT FAT	PROTEIN	CARBS
473	14.3g	7.6g	16.1g	61.2g

COOK'S TIP

Choose how much heat you want. Deseed the green chilli before chopping for milder heat or go all out and swirl a little fresh chilli paste into your bowl.

★★★★★ *This slightly spicy soup is delicious and very easy to make in the slow cooker.* **AUSSIE_IDA**

● EASY ● FAMILY-FRIENDLY ○ GLUTEN FREE ○ LOW CAL ○ QUICK ● FREEZABLE

SLOW PHO BO

BEEF

Lots of ingredients, but this gluten-free soup is pretty quick to prep for the slow cooker before you forget about it for the day. You'll devour the result!

SERVES 6 **PREP** 20 mins (+ 1 hour soaking) **COOK** 10 hours 10 mins

1.2kg meaty beef bones or oxtail
1½ tbs sea salt
8 whole cloves
4 whole star anise
2 tsp whole coriander seeds
1 tsp fennel seeds
2 tsp cumin seeds
2 tsp peppercorns
2 brown onions, quartered
2 large carrots, peeled, cut
   into 5cm pieces
5 garlic cloves, peeled, bruised
8cm-piece fresh ginger, peeled,
   cut into 2cm pieces
2 cinnamon sticks
2 tbs fish sauce, plus extra, to taste
15g palm sugar, grated
2 tbs fresh lime juice
250g pkt flat rice noodles
250g fillet steak, very thinly sliced
200g bean sprouts, trimmed
3 green shallots, thinly sliced
2 long fresh red chillies, thinly sliced
1½ cups mixed fresh herbs (see tip)
Gluten-free hoisin sauce and lime
   wedges, to serve

1 Place bones and 1 tbs salt in a large bowl. Cover with water. Set aside for 1 hour to soak. Drain. Rinse under cold running water. Transfer to a slow cooker.

2 Meanwhile, wrap the cloves, star anise, coriander, fennel, cumin and peppercorns in a small piece of muslin and secure with unwaxed white kitchen string.

3 Place the onion, carrot, garlic, ginger, cinnamon, fish sauce, palm sugar, remaining salt and the spice pouch in the slow cooker. Add enough water to cover the meat. Cover and cook on Low for 8-10 hours or until beef is falling from the bones.

4 Use a slotted spoon to transfer solids to a bowl. Discard vegetables and spice pouch. Remove meat from bones and shred. Discard bones. Skim and discard fat from the surface of the stock. Stir in lime juice and shredded beef. Add extra fish sauce, to taste. Keep warm.

5 Place noodles in a heatproof bowl. Cover with boiling water. Stand for 5-10 minutes or until just tender. Drain. Divide noodles and soup among serving bowls. Top with sliced beef, bean sprouts, shallot, chilli and herbs. Serve with hoisin sauce and lime wedges.

COOK'S TIP

We used a mix of fresh coriander, Vietnamese mint and Thai basil leaves to top this soup.

NUTRITION (PER SERVE)

CALS	FAT	SAT FAT	PROTEIN	CARBS
423	11g	4g	31g	43g

○ EASY   ○ FAMILY-FRIENDLY   ● GLUTEN FREE   ● LOW CAL   ○ QUICK   ○ FREEZABLE

20+ *minutes prep*

★★★★★

This is a stunner of a recipe that produces a delicious pho. Easy to do. **EMMABARLOW**

PORK & BEAN SOUPY
GOULASH

Packed full of classic soup root vegies, this Hungarian-style feast boasts a hint of smokiness that matches the pork beautifully.

SERVES 6　**PREP** 30 mins　**COOK** 1 hour 55 mins

1½ tsp caraway seeds
250g smoked streaky bacon,
　thinly sliced
3 pork loin cutlets, trimmed, cut into
　1.5cm pieces, bones reserved
2 brown onions, finely chopped
2 celery sticks, finely chopped, plus
　1 cup leaves, finely chopped
3 garlic cloves, crushed
2 tbs Hungarian sweet paprika
1 tbs hot smoked paprika,
　plus extra, to serve
2 large ripe tomatoes, chopped
2 tsp fresh thyme leaves
1L (4 cups) salt-reduced
　chicken stock
1 red capsicum, deseeded, chopped
1 turnip, peeled, chopped
2 carrots, peeled, chopped
2 potatoes, peeled, chopped
400g can cannellini beans,
　rinsed, drained
80g chopped kale or baby kale leaves
Sour cream, baby herbs and crusty
　rye bread, to serve

1 Heat a large flameproof casserole dish over medium-low heat. Add caraway seeds. Cook, stirring, for 1-2 minutes or until aromatic. Transfer to a bowl. Add the bacon. Cook, stirring, for 3-4 minutes or until crispy. Use a slotted spoon to transfer to a separate bowl, reserving fat in pan.

2 Season pork. Heat the bacon fat over medium heat. Cook pork in 2 batches, turning, for 3-4 minutes or until browned. Add onion and celery. Cook, stirring, for 3 minutes or until softened. Stir in garlic for 1 minute or until aromatic. Add sweet paprika, hot paprika and toasted caraway seeds. Cook, stirring, for 1 minute or until aromatic. Stir in tomato, celery leaves and thyme. Add stock, 500ml (2 cups) water and reserved bones. Bring to the boil. Reduce heat to low. Simmer for 45 minutes or until pork is tender.

3 Add capsicum, turnip, carrot and potato. Simmer for 35-40 minutes or until tender. Season well. Remove bones and discard. Stir in beans and kale for 2 minutes or until kale just wilts. Ladle soup among serving bowls. Top with sour cream. Sprinkle with extra paprika and herbs. Serve with the rye bread.

COOK'S TIP

Making this soup gluten-free is easy. Simply use gluten-free stock, and either omit the bread or go for a gluten-free variety.

NUTRITION (PER SERVE)

CALS	FAT	SAT FAT	PROTEIN	CARBS
503	19.8g	8.3g	38.5g	40g

○ EASY　● FAMILY-FRIENDLY　○ GLUTEN FREE　○ LOW CAL　○ QUICK　● FREEZABLE

PEA & SMOKED HAM

This slow-cooker pea and ham soup has a delicious apple and parsnip twist that will keep you coming back bowl after bowl.

SERVES 6 **PREP** 20 mins **COOK** 8 hours 5 mins

1 tbs extra virgin olive oil, plus extra, to drizzle

1 brown onion, coarsely chopped

2 tsp ground cumin

1kg smoked ham hock

4 parsnips, peeled, chopped

2 green apples, peeled, cored, coarsely chopped

530g (2½ cups) green split peas

1 large lemon, rind finely grated, plus extra shredded rind, to serve

Crème fraîche and fresh mint leaves, to serve

1 Heat the oil in a small frying pan over high heat. Add the onion and cook, stirring, for 5 minutes or until softened. Stir in the cumin and cook for 30 seconds or until aromatic. Transfer the mixture to a slow cooker.

2 Add the ham hock, parsnip, apple, split peas and 2L (8 cups) water to the slow cooker. Stir well. Cover. Cook on High for 6-8 hours or until ham is very tender.

3 Use tongs or a slotted spoon to transfer the ham hock to a clean board. Use a stick blender to blend the soup in the slow cooker until smooth, adding up to 250ml (1 cup) extra water if the mixture is too thick. Stir in the lemon rind.

4 Use fingers to remove the ham from the hock, discarding the bone, skin and fat. Ladle the soup among serving bowls. Top with crème fraîche, ham, mint and lemon rind. Drizzle with extra oil and season with pepper, to serve

COOK'S TIP

Replace 2 of the parsnips with 2 carrots, if you prefer.

NUTRITION (PER SERVE)

CALS	FAT	SAT FAT	PROTEIN	CARBS
573	18g	6g	38g	55g

● EASY ● FAMILY-FRIENDLY ● GLUTEN FREE ○ LOW CAL ○ QUICK ● FREEZABLE

VEGIE GOODNESS

HAIL THE KALE AND ALL KINDS OF OTHER HEALTHY LEAF
AND ROOT VEG IN SOUP BOWLS YOU'LL WANT TO DEVOUR.

CREAMY CAULIFLOWER & KALE

A low-cal, super-nutritious veg soup to dive your spoon into.
Kale is a superstar, high in A, C and K vitamins, plus iron and calcium.

SERVES 6 **PREP** 15 mins (+ cooling) **COOK** 45 mins

1 tbs extra virgin olive oil,
 plus extra, to serve

20g butter

1 small brown onion, finely chopped

2 garlic cloves, chopped

1 head (about 750g) cauliflower,
 chopped

1.5L (6 cups) gluten-free chicken
 or vegetable stock

140g pkt chopped kale leaves

80ml (⅓ cup) thickened cream,
 plus extra, to serve

1 tbs pepitas, lightly toasted

20g (¼ cup) finely grated parmesan

1 Heat the oil and butter in a large saucepan over medium heat. Add the onion and garlic. Cook, stirring often, for 5 minutes or until softened.

2 Add the cauliflower and stock. Cover. Bring to the boil. Reduce heat to low. Simmer, covered, for 15 minutes or until cauliflower is tender.

3 Add the kale and increase the heat to high. Bring to the boil then reduce the heat to medium-low. Simmer, uncovered, for 15 minutes or until the kale is wilted. Remove from the heat and set aside for 10 minutes to cool slightly.

4 Use a stick blender to blend soup in pan until smooth. Stir in the cream. Place over medium heat and cook, stirring occasionally, for 5 minutes or until heated through. Ladle soup among serving bowls. Drizzle over extra cream and oil. Top with pepitas and parmesan. Season and serve.

COOK'S TIP

To make this dish dairy free, replace the butter with 1 tbs extra virgin olive oil, the parmesan with toasted coconut flakes and the cream with coconut cream.

NUTRITION (PER SERVE)

CALS	FAT	SAT FAT	PROTEIN	CARBS
232	18.9g	8.5g	6.5g	8.2g

★★★★★ *This was surprisingly good! I would make it again, as I have a lot of kale in the garden.* **NEATO**

● EASY ○ FAMILY-FRIENDLY ● GLUTEN FREE ● LOW CAL ○ QUICK ● FREEZABLE

SPICED CHICKPEA & QUINOA VEGIE

The spices just seem to melt into the pumpkin and cauliflower, and into your heart, ensuring this more-ish bowl becomes a dinner favourite.

SERVES 4 **PREP** 15 mins **COOK** 40 mins

1 tbs extra virgin olive oil
1 brown onion, halved, sliced
1 carrot, halved, sliced
1 celery stalk, sliced
2 garlic cloves, crushed
2 tsp curry powder
2 tsp garam masala
1L (4 cups) vegetable stock
70g (⅓ cup) tricolour quinoa, rinsed
½ small cauliflower, cut into
    small florets
300g butternut pumpkin,
    cut into 1cm pieces
300g can chickpeas, rinsed, drained
130g (½ cup) plain Greek-style
    yoghurt
2 tbs chopped fresh coriander
    leaves, plus extra sprigs, to serve
2 tbs pepitas, toasted

1 Heat the oil in a large saucepan over medium heat. Add the onion, carrot, celery and garlic. Cook, stirring, for 5 minutes or until onion is softened. Add the curry powder and garam masala. Cook, stirring, for 1 minute or until aromatic.

2 Add the stock and 500ml (2 cups) water. Bring to the boil. Stir in the quinoa. Reduce heat to low. Simmer, covered, for 20 minutes. Add the cauliflower, pumpkin and chickpeas. Simmer, covered, for 10 minutes or until vegetables are tender.

3 Season. Combine yoghurt and chopped coriander in a bowl. Serve soup topped with coriander yoghurt, pepitas and extra coriander sprigs.

COOK'S TIP

You can freeze the soup at the end of step 2. Place in an airtight container and freeze for up to 3 months. Thaw in the fridge overnight before continuing with step 3.

NUTRITION (PER SERVE)

CALS	FAT	SAT FAT	PROTEIN	CARBS
307	12.6g	3.2g	10.7g	36.4g

● EASY ● FAMILY-FRIENDLY ○ GLUTEN FREE ● LOW CAL ○ QUICK ● FREEZABLE

★ ★ ★ ★ ★

So hearty, my meat-eaters didn't even miss the meat! CMON

15
minutes
prep

ULTIMATE VEGETARIAN RAMEN

Nice and easy, this ramen dinner bowl is loaded with noodles, pumpkin and mushrooms in a hearty vegetable broth.

SERVES 4 **PREP** 15 mins **COOK** 25 mins

2 tsp honey
2 tsp vegetable oil
75g (¼ cup) white miso paste
60ml (¼ cup) light soy sauce
500g kent pumpkin, deseeded, left unpeeled, thinly sliced
4 eggs
1.5L (6 cups) vegetable stock
20g dried whole shiitake mushrooms
2 tsp finely grated fresh ginger
1 bunch buk choy, sliced
2 small carrots, peeled, thinly sliced
450g shelf-fresh ramen noodles
2 green shallots, thinly sliced
2 tsp sesame seeds, toasted
Dried chilli flakes and thinly shredded nori, to serve (optional)

1 Preheat oven to 200°C/180°C fan forced. Line a baking tray with baking paper. Whisk the honey, oil, 1 tbs miso and 1 tbs soy sauce in a small bowl.

2 Arrange the pumpkin on the prepared tray and brush both sides with miso mixture. Roast for 15-20 minutes or until tender.

3 Meanwhile, place the eggs in a saucepan and cover with water. Bring to the boil over high heat. As soon as the water boils, cook for 2 minutes. Drain and refresh under cold running water. Peel and halve.

4 Place the stock, mushrooms, ginger and remaining soy sauce in a large saucepan. Cover. Bring to a simmer over medium heat. Add buk choy stems and carrot. Simmer for 2 minutes or until tender-crisp. Remove from heat. Stir in remaining miso until dissolved. Add noodles and buk choy leaves. Set aside for 1 minute or until noodles are warmed through and leaves are tender.

5 Ladle the soup among serving bowls. Top with pumpkin, egg, shallot, sesame seeds, and chilli and nori, if using.

COOK'S TIP

You'll find miso paste, dried shiitake mushrooms and the noodles in the Asian section of most large supermarkets.

NUTRITION (PER SERVE)

CALS	FAT	SAT FAT	PROTEIN	CARBS
403	11.9g	2.6g	19.8g	49.5g

● EASY ○ FAMILY-FRIENDLY ○ GLUTEN FREE ● LOW CAL ○ QUICK ○ FREEZABLE

SUPER BEETROOT & POTATO

Load up with antioxidants and vitamins in the shape of bright beetroot!
At it's best in cooler months, be sure to make this beaut bowl a winter staple.

SERVES 4 **PREP** 15 mins **COOK** 30 mins

1 tbs olive oil
1 brown onion, chopped
2 garlic cloves, crushed
1kg beetroot, peeled, chopped
250g potatoes, peeled,
   finely chopped
1L (4 cups) gluten-free
   vegetable stock
Sour cream, fresh dill sprigs
   and beetroot chips (optional),
   to serve

1 Heat the oil in a large saucepan over medium heat. Add the onion. Cook, stirring, for 5 minutes or until softened.

2 Stir the garlic, beetroot and potato into the pan. Stir in the stock. Cover and bring to a simmer. Cook for 20 minutes or until the beetroot is tender. Use a stick blender to blend soup in the pan until smooth.

3 Ladle soup among serving bowls. Top with sour cream and dill. Season. Serve with beetroot chips, if you like.

COOK'S TIP

You can add a chopped carrot or 2 to increase the vegie content, if you like. It will also make the soup slightly sweeter, which might be more appealing to kids.

NUTRITION (PER SERVE)

CALS	FAT	SAT FAT	PROTEIN	CARBS
305	14.5g	5.8g	7.5g	31.5g

★★★★★ *Our family really loves this soup.*
We like to serve it with crusty wholegrain bread for mopping up. **RILEYBEAR**

● EASY ● FAMILY-FRIENDLY ● GLUTEN FREE ● LOW CAL ○ QUICK ● FREEZABLE

187

SPICY BLACK BEAN & CORN

This spicy, satisfying vegetarian soup is healthy, too. It's rich in antioxidants, protein and fibre, thanks to all those delicious black beans and more.

SERVES 4 **PREP** 15 mins **COOK** 8 hours 10 min

- 220g (1 cup) dried black beans, rinsed, drained
- 2 tsp extra virgin olive oil
- 1 large brown onion, finely chopped
- 2 celery sticks, finely chopped
- 2 garlic cloves, crushed
- 2 tsp ground cumin
- 2 tsp sweet paprika
- ½ tsp dried chilli flakes
- 400g can crushed tomatoes
- 300g sweet potato, peeled, chopped
- 1 large sweet corncob, kernels removed
- 2 tbs chopped fresh coriander leaves
- 1 long fresh green chilli, deseeded, finely chopped
- Lime wedges, to serve

1. Place the black beans in a large saucepan. Cover with enough water to come 5cm above beans. Bring to the boil over medium-high heat. Cook for 10 minutes. Drain well.

2. Meanwhile, heat the oil in a large non-stick frying pan over medium heat. Add the onion and celery. Cook, stirring, for 5 minutes or until softened. Add the garlic, cumin, paprika and chilli. Cook, stirring, for 1 minute or until aromatic. Transfer to a slow cooker. Add the beans, tomato and 1.25L (5 cups) water (see tip). Cover. Cook on Low for 7 hours.

3. Add the sweet potato and corn. Cook for a further 1 hour or until potato is tender and soup is thickened. Season.

4. Combine the coriander and chilli in a bowl. Ladle soup among serving bowls. Top with the coriander mixture. Serve with lime wedges.

COOK'S TIP

If you like a little more seasoning in your soups, you can swap the 1.25L water for vegetable or chicken stock, gluten-free if needed.

NUTRITION (PER SERVE)

CALS	FAT	SAT FAT	PROTEIN	CARBS
346	14g	2g	21g	29g

● EASY ● FAMILY-FRIENDLY ● GLUTEN FREE ● LOW CAL ○ QUICK ● FREEZABLE

15 minutes prep

★★★★★ *This is a fantastic, nutritious soup. The lime, coriander and chilli at the end make it burst with flavour.* **MAREE_K**

ROAST CARROT & CORIANDER PESTO

Sweet and creamy from the roasted carrots, plus a zesty boost from the coriander pesto topper – this soup has it all.

SERVES 4 **PREP** 20 mins **COOK** 1 hour

1kg carrots, peeled, coarsely chopped
2 tbs olive oil, plus extra, to drizzle
1 brown onion, coarsely chopped
3 garlic cloves, crushed
2 tsp ground cumin
1L (4 cups) gluten-free beef stock
1 tbs coriander seeds, toasted, slightly crushed

CORIANDER PESTO
½ cup fresh coriander leaves
45g (¼ cup) raw unsalted macadamias
1 garlic clove, crushed
2 tbs shredded parmesan
2 tbs extra virgin olive oil, plus extra 1-2 tbs
1 tbs fresh lemon juice

1 Preheat oven to 200°C/180°C fan forced. Line a baking tray with baking paper. Place carrots on prepared tray. Drizzle with half the oil. Season. Roast, turning halfway through cooking, for 30-35 minutes or until tender.

2 Meanwhile, to make the pesto, place the coriander, macadamias, garlic and parmesan in a food processor. Process until finely chopped. With the motor running, add the oil in a thin steady stream until well combined. Add the lemon juice and process until well combined. Stir through enough extra oil to reach the desired consistency.

3 Heat the remaining 1 tbs oil in a large saucepan over medium-high heat. Add the onion and cook, stirring, for 5 minutes or until softened. Add the garlic and cumin. Cook, stirring, for 30 seconds or until aromatic. Add the carrot and stock. Bring to the boil. Simmer for 15 minutes. Remove from heat.

4 Use a stick blender to blend soup in the pan until smooth. Season. Ladle soup among serving bowls. Swirl through the pesto. Drizzle with extra oil. Sprinkle with coriander seeds. Season with pepper and serve.

COOK'S TIP

Swap the pesto for a swirl of sour cream and a sprinkling of croutons for a change or kid-friendly topper.

NUTRITION (PER SERVE)

CALS	FAT	SAT FAT	PROTEIN	CARBS
463	38.2g	6.3g	5.7g	20.1g

● EASY ● FAMILY-FRIENDLY ● GLUTEN FREE ○ LOW CAL ○ QUICK ● FREEZABLE

★★★★★ *So healthy! Easy to make. Pesto is divine and the flavours blend beautifully with the soup.* **ZIGGYIZALCO**

CREAMY VEGAN TOMATO &
RAVIOLI

This easy vegan soup is filling and mega tasty. Better still, it can be prepped, cooked and on the table in just 40 minutes. Get your spoons ready!

SERVES 4 **PREP** 10 mins **COOK** 30 mins

1 tbs extra virgin olive oil, plus extra, to serve
1 brown onion, chopped
2 garlic cloves, chopped
800g can whole peeled tomatoes
1 large potato, peeled, chopped
500ml (2 cups) vegetable stock
1 tsp dried oregano
300g pkt vegan spinach and ricotta ravioli
250ml (1 cup) almond milk
150g baby spinach, plus extra, to serve
Fresh basil leaves, to serve

1 Heat the oil in a large saucepan over medium-high heat. Add the onion and garlic. Season. Cook, stirring occasionally, for 6 minutes or until softened. Add the tomato, potato, stock and oregano. Bring to the boil. Cover. Reduce heat to medium. Simmer for 20 minutes. Remove pan from the heat.

2 Meanwhile, cook the pasta in salted boiling water following packet directions. Drain well.

3 Stir almond milk into the soup mixture. Using a stick blender, blend mixture in the pan until smooth. Add the spinach and stir until starting to wilt.

4 Ladle soup among serving bowls. Top with the pasta, extra spinach and basil. Drizzle with a little extra oil. Season with pepper and serve.

COOK'S TIP

If you're not following a vegan diet, feel free to swap the ravioli for any flavour of ravioli or tortellini you desire.

NUTRITION (PER SERVE)

CALS	FAT	SAT FAT	PROTEIN	CARBS
319	8.6g	1.3g	8.5g	46.9g

★★★★★ *I knew this would be a new family favourite and it went down like a treat!* **TRACEY1901**

● EASY ● FAMILY-FRIENDLY ○ GLUTEN FREE ● LOW CAL ○ QUICK ● FREEZABLE

CREAMY BORLOTTI BEAN &
PASTA

A bowlful of comfort! Vegetarians and meat fanciers alike are certain to ask for a second serving of this heavenly bean and pasta dinner.

SERVES 4 **PREP** 10 mins **COOK** 35 mins

1 tbs extra virgin olive oil
1 brown onion, finely chopped
2 carrots, finely chopped
2 garlic cloves, finely chopped
1 tsp finely chopped fresh
    rosemary leaves
1L (4 cups) vegetable stock
400g can diced tomatoes
200g dried spiral pasta
400g can borlotti beans,
    rinsed, drained
125ml (½ cup) thickened cream
2 tbs shaved parmesan
2 tbs coarsely chopped fresh
    continental parsley leaves

1 Heat the oil in a large saucepan over medium-high heat. Add the onion, carrot, garlic and rosemary. Cook, stirring, for 5 minutes or until onion is softened. Stir in the stock and tomato. Bring to the boil. Reduce heat to medium. Cook, covered, for 10 minutes. Remove from the heat.

2 Use a stick blender to blend soup in the pan until smooth. Season. Return to the boil over medium-high heat. Stir in pasta. Simmer, covered, stirring occasionally, for 12-15 minutes or until pasta is just tender. Stir in the beans and half the cream.

3 Ladle soup among serving bowls. Swirl through the remaining cream. Top with the parmesan and parsley. Season with pepper and serve.

COOK'S TIP

This soup would be even more delicious with a dollop of pesto on top before serving. If you have some on hand, try it!

NUTRITION (PER SERVE)

CALS	FAT	SAT FAT	PROTEIN	CARBS
476	19.6g	9.5g	14.5g	59g

★★★★★ *So easy and hardly any washing up. Most ingredients are already in the pantry.* **SNODDY88**

● EASY ● FAMILY-FRIENDLY ○ GLUTEN FREE ○ LOW CAL ○ QUICK ● FREEZABLE

PUMPKIN, HALOUMI BITES &
CROUTONS

Stay cosy with this loaded pumpkin soup, complete with crispy garlic croutons and salty haloumi. This one is definitely a keeper!

SERVES 4 **PREP** 15 mins **COOK** 25 mins

60ml (¼ cup) extra virgin
   olive oil, plus extra, to serve
1 brown onion, chopped
1kg butternut pumpkin, peeled,
   chopped
1 potato, peeled, chopped
500ml (2 cups) vegetable stock
2 slices white bread
2 garlic cloves, thinly sliced
4 fresh thyme sprigs, plus extra,
   to serve
180g pkt haloumi, cut into
   5mm cubes
2 tbs pepitas, toasted
Coarsely chopped fresh continental
   parsley leaves, to serve

1 Heat 1 tbs oil in a large saucepan over medium-high heat. Add the onion and pumpkin. Season. Cook, stirring occasionally, for 5 minutes or until onion is softened. Add the potato, stock and 250ml (1 cup) water. Bring to the boil. Cover. Reduce heat to medium-high. Simmer gently for 15 minutes or until vegies are tender. Remove pan from heat.

2 Meanwhile, remove and discard crust from the bread. Cut into 5mm cubes.

3 Heat remaining oil in a large frying pan over medium-high heat. Add garlic and thyme. Cook, stirring, for 2 minutes or until golden and aromatic. Using a slotted spoon, transfer to a plate. Add bread to pan. Cook, stirring, for 5 minutes or until golden and crisp. Using a slotted spoon, transfer to a plate lined with paper towel. Add haloumi to the pan. Cook, tossing occasionally, for 2-3 minutes or until golden.

4 Use a stick blender to blend soup in pan until smooth. Season. Ladle soup among serving bowls. Top with the croutons, garlic mixture, haloumi, pepitas, extra thyme and the parsley. Drizzle with extra oil. Season with pepper. Serve.

COOK'S TIP

A nice hearty sourdough makes great croutons, but any type of bread will do.

NUTRITION (PER SERVE)

CALS	FAT	SAT FAT	PROTEIN	CARBS
536	35.2g	11.5g	18.8g	32.1g

○ EASY ● FAMILY-FRIENDLY ○ GLUTEN FREE ○ LOW CAL ○ QUICK ● FREEZABLE

15
*minutes
prep*

SPEEDY WINTER
MINESTRONE

We think minestrone is the perfect mid-week soup – it uses pantry staples, it's fast and it's healthy. Here's our quick take on it.

SERVES 4 **PREP** 5 mins **COOK** 25 mins

500g tray roast mixed vegetables with garlic and rosemary (see tip)
2 tbs olive oil, plus extra, to drizzle
1 leek, halved, thinly sliced
1 tbs tomato paste
1L (4 cups) vegetable stock
400g can diced tomatoes
400g can borlotti beans, rinsed, drained
80g dried thin spaghetti, broken
60g pkt baby kale
4 slices sourdough bread
1 garlic clove, halved

1 Remove the garlic from the vegie tray and crush. Heat the oil in a large saucepan over medium heat. Add the leek, garlic and rosemary sprig from the tray. Cook, stirring, for 3 minutes or until aromatic. Add remaining veg from tray. Cook, stirring, for 3 minutes or until just starting to soften. Add the tomato paste. Cook, stirring, for 1 minute.

2 Add the stock and tomato. Cover. Bring to the boil. Simmer for 5 minutes or until vegies soften further. Add beans and pasta. Cook, stirring occasionally, for 8 minutes or until pasta is al dente. Add kale. Cook, stirring, until wilted.

3 Toast bread. Rub with garlic clove. Drizzle with extra oil and season. Serve soup with the garlic toast.

COOK'S TIP

Look for pre-prepared vegie trays in the fresh food section of the supermarket – they are great time savers. Or use a 500g mix of chopped sweet potato, potato, carrot and red onion, plus a garlic clove and sprig of rosemary.

NUTRITION (PER SERVE)

CALS	FAT	SAT FAT	PROTEIN	CARBS
475	16.7g	2.8g	15.4g	62.5g

★★★★★

A great soup when you want comfort food in a hurry. **SHAWNTHEPRAWN**

● EASY ● FAMILY-FRIENDLY ○ GLUTEN FREE ○ LOW CAL ● QUICK ○ FREEZABLE

5
minutes
prep

POTATO, CAULIFLOWER & CARROT

We blitzed three favourite vegies with stock and aromatics, stirred in some cream and then served it up with an onion crouton topper. Wow!

SERVES 6 **PREP** 15 mins **COOK** 50 mins

1 tbs extra virgin olive oil

1 medium leek, trimmed, halved, sliced

1kg carrots, peeled, chopped

500g cauliflower, trimmed, cut into florets

350g white potatoes, peeled, chopped

2 garlic cloves, crushed

1L (4 cups) chicken stock

Vegetable oil, to shallow fry

1 small red onion, halved, very thinly sliced

1 tbs plain flour

125ml (½ cup) pure cream

Chopped fresh chives, to serve (optional)

1 Heat the olive oil in a large saucepan over medium heat. Add the leek and cook, stirring, for 5 minutes or until softened. Add the carrot, cauliflower and potato. Cook, stirring occasionally, for 5 minutes.

2 Add the garlic. Cook, stirring for 1 minute or until aromatic. Stir in the stock and 500ml (2 cups) water. Season. Cover. Increase heat to high. Bring to the boil. Reduce heat to low. Simmer for 30 minutes or until vegetables are tender.

3 Add enough vegetable oil in a frying pan to come 1cm up side of pan. Heat over medium-high heat. Toss onion in flour. Cook, in batches, for 2-3 minutes or until golden. Drain on a plate lined with paper towel.

4 Use a stick blender to blend soup in the pan until smooth. Place pan over low heat. Stir in cream. Cook for 5 minutes or until heated through. Serve topped with onion croutons and chives (if using).

COOK'S TIP

Use vegetable stock instead of chicken for a vegetarian version of this soup.

NUTRITION (PER SERVE)

CALS	FAT	SAT FAT	PROTEIN	CARBS
262	13.5g	5.7g	6.8g	19.4g

● EASY ● FAMILY-FRIENDLY ○ GLUTEN FREE ● LOW CAL ○ QUICK ● FREEZABLE

★★★★★
Loved the soup – would make it again.
The family also enjoyed it.
Very easy to make. **PAM007**

15
minutes
prep

SPRING VEGIE WITH WHIPPED FETA

A lighter pasta soup that makes the most of seasonal spring vegetables. The whipped lemon feta gives it a very welcome tangy twist.

SERVES 4 **PREP** 10 mins **COOK** 20 mins

1 tbs extra virgin olive oil

3 garlic cloves, crushed

1L (4 cups) salt-reduced chicken stock

140g (1½ cups) dried wagon wheel pasta (see tip)

400g can cannellini beans, rinsed, drained

2 zucchini, cut into 1cm pieces

1 leek, trimmed, thinly sliced

1 bunch asparagus, trimmed, thinly sliced diagonally

120g (¾ cup) frozen peas

100g feta

2 tbs lemon juice

¼ cup finely chopped fresh continental parsley

1 tbs finely grated fresh lemon rind

1 Heat the oil in a large saucepan over medium-high heat. Add the garlic and cook, stirring, for 30 seconds or until aromatic. Add the stock and 740ml (3 cups) water. Bring to the boil.

2 Add the pasta. Return to the boil. Cook for 5 minutes. Add the beans, zucchini, leek and asparagus. Reduce heat to low. Simmer, adding peas in the last 2 minutes, for 5-6 minutes or until pasta and vegies are tender.

3 Meanwhile, blend the feta and lemon juice in a small food processor until smooth, adding a little water, if needed. Season with pepper.

4 Stir parsley through the soup. Serve soup topped with a dollop of whipped feta and a sprinkle of the lemon rind and pepper.

COOK'S TIP

The wagon wheel pasta looks very pretty in this soup, but you can use any short pasta you like.

NUTRITION (PER SERVE)

CALS	FAT	SAT FAT	PROTEIN	CARBS
402	12.3g	5g	20.3g	45.7g

★★★★★ *It was light and fresh, and extremely easy to bring together – perfect for a hot spring day.* **LADYKATIA1**

● EASY ● FAMILY-FRIENDLY ○ GLUTEN FREE ● LOW CAL ● QUICK ○ FREEZABLE

VEGETARIAN VIETNAMESE PHO

Everyone's favourite rice-noodle soup – pho – is now vegetarian and is just as soul-soothing as the beef version. Put it on the menu.

SERVES 4 **PREP** 15 mins **COOK** 4 hours 25 mins

250g dried rice vermicelli noodles
1 bunch baby pak choy, quartered lengthways
300g firm tofu, cut into 1.5cm pieces
Bean sprouts, fresh Vietnamese mint sprigs, sliced fresh red chilli, hot chilli sauce and lime wedges, to serve

VEGETABLE BROTH
2 cinnamon sticks
2 whole star anise
5 cloves
1½ tsp coriander seeds
1 tsp black peppercorns
1 large brown onion, quartered
5cm-piece ginger, peeled, halved horizontally
20g (¾ cup) sliced dried shiitake mushrooms
3L (12 cups) gluten-free vegetable stock
Light soy sauce, to taste

1 To make the broth, place the cinnamon, star anise, cloves, coriander seeds and peppercorns in a frying pan over medium heat. Cook, shaking the pan occasionally, for 2-3 minutes or until aromatic. Cool slightly. Transfer to a piece of muslin cloth and tie up with unwaxed kitchen string to make a pouch.

2 Add the onion and ginger to the pan. Cook over medium heat, stirring, for 3-5 minutes or until lightly charred.

3 Place the onion mixture, muslin pouch and mushroom in a slow cooker. Add the stock. Cover and cook on High for 4 hours to develop the flavours.

4 Place the noodles in a large heatproof bowl and cover with boiling water. Set aside for 5 minutes to soften. Drain well. Remove spice pouch from the broth. Stir in the soy sauce, to taste.

5 Add the pak choy and tofu to the slow cooker. Cover. Cook on High for 5-10 minutes or until the pak choy is tender. Divide noodles and soup among serving bowls. Top with bean sprouts, mint and sliced chilli. Serve with chilli sauce and lime wedges.

COOK'S TIP

Any leftover broth can be frozen in an airtight container for up to 3 months.

NUTRITION (PER SERVE)

CALS	FAT	SAT FAT	PROTEIN	CARBS
365	8g	2g	17g	52g

● EASY   ○ FAMILY-FRIENDLY   ● GLUTEN FREE   ● LOW CAL   ○ QUICK   ● FREEZABLE

15
*minutes
prep*

BLACK BEAN & CHIPOTLE

With four serves of veg per person, this super tasty Mexican-inspired vegie soup is gluten-free, plus low in fat and calories.

SERVES 4 **PREP** 20 mins **COOK** 35 mins

- 1 tbs extra virgin olive oil
- 1 large brown onion, finely chopped
- 2 celery sticks, finely chopped
- 2 carrots, peeled, finely chopped
- 2 garlic cloves, crushed
- 2 tsp smoked paprika
- 2 tsp ground cumin
- 1 tbs chipotle in adobo sauce
- 3 truss tomatoes, finely chopped
- 70g (⅓ cup) quinoa, rinsed
- 400g can black beans, rinsed, drained
- 500ml (2 cups) salt-reduced vegetable stock
- 1 large zucchini, thinly sliced
- 150g (1 cup) fresh corn kernels
- 1 tbs fresh lime juice, plus lime wedges, to serve
- ¼ cup chopped fresh coriander leaves, plus extra sprigs, to serve

1 Heat the oil in a large saucepan over medium heat. Add the onion, celery and carrot. Cook, stirring, for 5 minutes or until softened. Add the garlic, paprika, cumin and chipotle. Cook, stirring, for 1 minute or until aromatic. Add the tomato and cook, stirring occasionally, for 2-3 minutes or until starting to break down.

2 Add the quinoa, black beans, stock and 500ml (2 cups) water to the pan. Bring to the boil. Reduce heat to low. Simmer, partially covered, for 15 minutes or until the quinoa is tender.

3 Add the zucchini and corn to the pan. Simmer for 5 minutes or until vegetables are tender. Stir in the lime juice and coriander. Season. Ladle soup among serving bowls. Top with coriander sprigs. Serve with lime wedges.

NUTRITION (PER SERVE)

CALS	FAT	SAT FAT	PROTEIN	CARBS
305	7.5g	1g	13g	39g

COOK'S TIP

Chipotles are dried and smoked jalapeño chillies. They are available chopped in jars in a tangy sauce called adobo. You'll find them in the Mexican or international food section at the supermarket, or at specialty grocers.

★★★★★

Lovely warming soup, perfect for winter. **MELK83**

● EASY ○ FAMILY-FRIENDLY ● GLUTEN FREE ● LOW CAL ○ QUICK ● FREEZABLE

SPICED CAULIFLOWER & TAHINI

Warming and hearty, using tahini in this soup adds powerful antioxidants and healthy fats, as well as a delightful nutty flavour.

SERVES 4 **PREP** 15 mins **COOK** 1 hour 10 mins

1 head (1.2kg) cauliflower, trimmed
2½ tbs extra virgin olive oil, plus extra, to serve
1 brown onion, chopped
2 celery stalks, chopped
500g potatoes, peeled, chopped
¼ tsp chilli powder
1 tbs ground coriander
2 garlic cloves, quartered
500ml (2 cups) vegetable stock
75g (¼ cup) tahini
2 tbs pepitas
2 tsp sesame seeds
2 tbs fresh lemon juice
¼ cup chopped fresh coriander, plus extra leaves, to serve
2 Lebanese bread rounds, toasted, cut into wedges

1 Preheat oven to 220°C/200°C fan forced. Place whole cauliflower on a baking tray lined with baking paper. Drizzle with 1 tbs oil. Roast for 20 minutes or until golden and just tender. Stand for 2 minutes. Coarsely chop.

2 Heat 1 tbs remaining oil in a large saucepan over medium heat. Add onion. Cook, stirring, for 5 minutes or until starting to soften. Add celery, potato and cauliflower. Cook, stirring occasionally, for 10 minutes or until vegetables start to soften. Increase heat to high.

3 Add chilli, ground coriander and garlic to the pan. Cook, stirring, for 2 minutes or until aromatic. Stir in stock and 750ml (3 cups) water. Season. Cover. Bring to the boil. Reduce heat to low. Simmer, stirring occasionally, for 30 minutes or until potato is tender. Remove from heat. Stir in tahini. Use a stick blender to blend soup in the pan until smooth.

4 Heat the remaining oil in a small frying pan over medium-high heat. Cook pepitas and sesame seeds, stirring, for 2-3 minutes or until golden. Drain on paper towel.

5 Stir lemon juice and chopped coriander into soup. Ladle soup among serving bowls. Drizzle with oil. Sprinkle with pepita mixture and extra coriander. Serve with bread.

COOK'S TIP

To make up to 2 days ahead, complete recipe to the end of step 3. Store in an airtight container in the fridge. To serve, place soup in a saucepan over medium-high heat until hot, and continue with steps 4 and 5.

NUTRITION (PER SERVE)

CALS	FAT	SAT FAT	PROTEIN	CARBS
539	28.4g	3.9g	17g	48.3g

● EASY ● FAMILY-FRIENDLY ○ GLUTEN FREE ○ LOW CAL ○ QUICK ● FREEZABLE

MOROCCAN CARROT & GINGER

Make this hearty vegie soup your go-to in the cooler months. The red lentils are a good source of iron and magnesium and will fill you up nicely.

SERVES 4 **PREP** 10 mins **COOK** 30 mins

1 tbs extra virgin olive oil
2 large carrots, coarsely grated
1 brown onion, finely chopped
1 garlic clove, finely chopped
3cm-piece fresh ginger, peeled, finely chopped
1 tsp ground cumin
½ tsp ground cinnamon
Pinch of dried chilli flakes
1.5L (6 cups) gluten-free vegetable stock
375g pkt dried red lentils, rinsed
90g (⅓ cup) plain Greek-style yoghurt
2 tsp gluten-free pistachio dukkah
Chopped fresh continental parsley leaves, to serve

1 Heat the oil in a large saucepan over medium-high heat. Add the carrot, onion, garlic and ginger. Cook, stirring often, for 5 minutes or until onion is softened. Add the cumin, cinnamon and chilli. Stir to combine.

2 Add the stock and lentils to the pan. Bring to a simmer. Reduce heat to medium. Simmer for 20 minutes or until lentils are tender (see tip). Season.

3 Serve soup topped with yoghurt and sprinkled with the dukkah and parsley.

NUTRITION (PER SERVE)

CALS	FAT	SAT FAT	PROTEIN	CARBS
282	6.7g	1.4g	17.3g	32.4g

COOK'S TIP

If you find this soup is too thick when simmering, simply add a little water to thin it.

★★★★★

Delicious – entire family loved it and asked for more. **GRID58**

● EASY ● FAMILY-FRIENDLY ● GLUTEN FREE ● LOW CAL ○ QUICK ● FREEZABLE

CREAM OF ENGLISH SPINACH

We've topped this soup with golden feta croutons – need we say more?!
You'll want to savour the taste of every creamy dreamy spoonful.

SERVES 4 **PREP** 15 mins (+ cooling) **COOK** 35 mins

20g butter
1 small brown onion, chopped
1 garlic clove, crushed
2 medium cream delight potatoes,
   peeled, chopped
750ml (3 cups) vegetable stock
2 bunches English spinach, stems
   removed, leaves washed
80ml (⅓ cup) pure cream
Fresh basil leaves, to serve

FETA CROUTONS
100g feta, crumbled
2 tbs chopped fresh basil leaves
4 slices white bread
50g butter, softened

1 Melt the butter in a large saucepan over medium heat. Add the onion and garlic. Cook, stirring, for 5 minutes or until onion is softened. Add the potato, stock and 500ml (2 cups) of water. Bring to the boil. Reduce heat to low. Simmer, covered, for 20 minutes or until potato is tender. Add the spinach and cook, stirring, for 2 minutes or until spinach wilts. Cool for 10 minutes.

2 Meanwhile, to make the feta croutons, place feta and basil in a bowl. Season with pepper. Stir well to combine. Spread both sides of bread slices with butter. Divide the feta mixture between 2 buttered slices, pressing gently to compact. Top with remaining bread slices. Heat a frying pan over medium-high heat. Cook sandwiches for 1-2 minutes each side or until golden. Transfer to a chopping board. Cool for 2 minutes. Cut each sandwich into 8 squares.

3 Use a stick blender to blend soup in pan until smooth. Stir in the cream. Place soup over low heat. Stir for 5 minutes or until heated through. Season. Serve soup topped with croutons and basil.

COOK'S TIP

You could replace the feta with grated cheddar, if that is all you have on hand – still delicious!

NUTRITION (PER SERVE)

CALS	FAT	SAT FAT	PROTEIN	CARBS
453	29.8g	18.6g	13.1g	29.4g

● EASY ○ FAMILY-FRIENDLY ○ GLUTEN FREE ○ LOW CAL ○ QUICK ● FREEZABLE

★ ★ ★ ★ ★

Paired with the feta croutons, this soup was delicious. A nice winter warmer. **CUPCAKEAINA**

15+
*minutes
prep*

SUPER GREEN
COCONUT

This easy soup is low-cal, gluten-free and ready in just 20 minutes!
It's super satisfying for a light meal at any time of the year.

SERVES 4 **PREP** 10 mins **COOK** 10 mins

1 tbs olive oil, plus extra,
  to drizzle
3 green shallots, chopped
2cm-piece ginger, grated
1 garlic clove, coarsely chopped
230g (1½ cups) frozen peas
100g baby spinach, plus extra,
  to serve
400ml can light coconut milk
500ml (2 cups) gluten-free
  vegetable stock
½ cup fresh coriander sprigs,
  plus extra, to serve
Fried shallots and sliced fresh
  red chilli (optional), to serve

1 Heat the oil in a large saucepan over medium heat. Add the shallot, ginger and garlic. Cook, stirring, for 1 minute or until aromatic. Add the peas and spinach. Cook, stirring, for 2-3 minutes or until peas are just tender.

2 Reserve 1 tbs coconut milk. Add the stock, coriander sprigs and remaining coconut milk to the pan. Cook for 3 minutes (don't let it boil). Remove from the heat.

3 Use a stick blender to blend soup in the pan until smooth. Return to medium heat to warm through.

4 Ladle the soup among serving bowls. Drizzle with the reserved coconut milk and extra oil. Sprinkle with the extra coriander and baby spinach, fried shallots and sliced red chilli, if using.

COOK'S TIP

You could add other green vegies if you like, such as chopped zucchini or chopped broccoli. Add them with the peas and spinach in step 1.

NUTRITION (PER SERVE)

CALS	FAT	SAT FAT	PROTEIN	CARBS
229	18g	9g	6g	9g

★★★★★ *An easy soup to prepare and cook. Tasted yum; quite a 'light' soup as well and something different. A winner!* **SEB24258**

● EASY ○ FAMILY-FRIENDLY ● GLUTEN FREE ● LOW CAL ● QUICK ● FREEZABLE

SLOW-COOKED RED LENTIL

Just pop the ingredients in the slow cooker and then return several hours later to a hearty vegetarian meal. We just love set and forgets!

SERVES 4 **PREP** 20 mins **COOK** 4 hours 10 mins

2 tsp olive oil
1 brown onion, chopped
2 carrots, diced
2 celery stalks, chopped
2 garlic cloves, thinly sliced
4cm-piece fresh ginger, peeled, finely chopped
3 tsp ground cumin
3 tsp ground coriander
325g (1½ cups) dried red lentils
1L (4 cups) chicken or vegetable stock
Plain Greek-style yoghurt, fresh coriander leaves and warmed garlic naan bread, to serve

1 Heat the oil in a large non-stick frying pan over medium heat. Add the onion, carrot and celery. Cook, stirring often, for 5 minutes or until onion is softened. Add the garlic and ginger. Cook, stirring, for 1 minute or until aromatic. Add the cumin and coriander. Cook, stirring, for 30 seconds or until aromatic. Transfer to a slow cooker.

2 Add the lentils, stock and 500ml (2 cups) water. Season. Cover. Cook on Low for 4 hours or until thickened.

3 Ladle soup among serving bowls. Top with yoghurt and coriander. Season with pepper. Serve with naan bread.

COOK'S TIP

Don't be tempted to skip the first step and throw everything into the slow cooker. Cooking the vegies and other flavourings in oil for a few minutes makes all the difference.

NUTRITION (PER SERVE)

CALS	FAT	SAT FAT	PROTEIN	CARBS
696	13.9g	3.4g	34.3g	98.4g

★★★★★ *This is a fave for my 7-year-old vegetarian daughter – easy to make, very nutritious and freezes well for those busy evenings after sport, etc.* **CASSIEB1977**

● EASY ● FAMILY-FRIENDLY ○ GLUTEN FREE ○ LOW CAL ○ QUICK ● FREEZABLE

ROASTED TOMATO & CAPSICUM

Oh so wonderfully rich and slurpable, this rosy red soup is just made for dunking big chunks of crusty bread into. Spoons are optional!

SERVES 4 **PREP** 15 mins (+ cooling) **COOK** 2 hours 10 mins

1 garlic bulb
1.5kg ripe roma tomatoes, halved lengthways
2 red onions, halved
2 tbs extra virgin olive oil
2 large red capsicums, quartered, deseeded
1L (4 cups) vegetable stock
60g goat's cheese, crumbled
¼ cup fresh basil leaves
Crusty bread, to serve

1 Preheat oven to 150°C/130°C fan forced. Line 2 large baking trays with baking paper.

2 Trim top quarter from the garlic bulb. Place the tomato, cut-side up, plus the onion and garlic, on 1 prepared baking tray. Place the capsicum on the second tray. Drizzle all veg with the oil. Roast for 2 hours or until tomato has collapsed. Cool for 10 minutes.

3 Place the tomato, onion, capsicum and half the stock in a food processor. Squeeze garlic from skins and add to the processor. Process for 3-4 minutes or until smooth.

4 Transfer tomato mixture to a large saucepan. Pour in the remaining stock. Cook over medium-high heat for 5 minutes or until heated through. Season. Ladle among serving bowls. Top with goat's cheese and basil. Season and serve with bread.

COOK'S TIP

Roasting the vegies adds an amazing depth of flavour to this soup, and is well worth the time – which is mostly unattended anyway!

NUTRITION (PER SERVE)

CALS	FAT	SAT FAT	PROTEIN	CARBS
457	15.8g	4.7g	15.8g	59.5g

★★★★★ *Very yummy and easy to make. A great twist on the typical tomato soup recipe.* **MINIMUMZEE**

● EASY ● FAMILY-FRIENDLY ○ GLUTEN FREE ○ LOW CAL ○ QUICK ● FREEZABLE

15+
minutes
prep

BUCKWHEAT & MUSHROOM

Looking for a substantial vegetarian meal to get you through? Look no further. Half a kilo of mushrooms and fibre-rich buckwheat ought to do it!

SERVES 4 **PREP** 15 mins **COOK** 35 mins

1 tbs extra virgin olive oil
1 brown onion, finely chopped
3 garlic cloves, finely chopped
500g flat mushrooms, finely chopped
125ml (½ cup) red wine (see tip)
1.25L (5 cups) chicken or
   vegetable stock
110g (½ cup) buckwheat, toasted
3 small fresh or dried bay leaves
100g baby spinach
¼ cup chopped fresh dill
Plain Greek-style yoghurt
   and paprika, to serve

1 Heat the oil in a large saucepan over medium heat. Add the onion and cook, stirring often, for 5 minutes or until softened. Add the garlic. Cook, stirring, for 1 minute or until aromatic. Add the mushroom and stir to coat. Pour in the wine and simmer for 2 minutes or until the liquid has reduced slightly.

2 Stir in the stock, buckwheat and bay leaves. Simmer, uncovered, for 25 minutes or until the buckwheat is tender. Stir through the spinach and 2 tbs dill. Season.

3 Ladle soup among serving bowls. Top with a dollop of yoghurt, the remaining dill and a sprinkle of paprika.

COOK'S TIP

If you would rather skip the wine, just increase the stock by 125ml (½ cup).

NUTRITION (PER SERVE)

CALS	FAT	SAT FAT	PROTEIN	CARBS
241	8g	2g	9g	21g

● EASY ○ FAMILY-FRIENDLY ○ GLUTEN FREE ● LOW CAL ○ QUICK ○ FREEZABLE

★★★★★

This really is a meal in a bowl. So good, so filling. **JGILLIS**

SWEET POTATO & CHILLI CREAM

Sweetness loves spice, so the secret in this warming vegie soup is a spoonful of Thai curry paste, plus a creamy chilli topping.

SERVES 4 **PREP** 15 mins **COOK** 40 mins

2 tsp sunflower oil
1 large brown onion, finely chopped
1 tbs red curry paste
2 carrots, peeled, thickly sliced
750g sweet potato, peeled,
   coarsely chopped
1L (4 cups) chicken stock
2 tsp fresh lime juice
½ tsp brown sugar
90g (⅓ cup) extra light sour cream
1 long fresh red chilli,
   finely chopped
1 tbs chopped fresh coriander
   leaves

1 Heat the oil in a large saucepan over medium heat. Cook the onion for 5 minutes or until softened. Stir in the curry paste for 1-2 minutes or until aromatic.

2 Add the carrot, sweet potato and stock. Bring to the boil. Reduce heat to low. Simmer for 25-30 minutes or until tender. Cool slightly.

3 Use a stick blender to blend the soup in the pan until smooth. Place over a low heat for 2-3 minutes. Stir in the lime juice and brown sugar. Season.

4 Combine the sour cream, chilli and coriander in a bowl. Serve with the soup.

NUTRITION (PER SERVE)

CALS	FAT	SAT FAT	PROTEIN	CARBS
221	5.5g	2g	6.5g	37g

COOK'S TIP

Sweet potato is a good source of dietary fibre, several carotenoids that act as antioxidants, plus it is high in vitamins C, E and betacarotene.

★★★★★ *A winner! Perfectly simple and really tasty. Great on its own but even better with the chilli cream.* **WINNS**

● EASY ○ FAMILY-FRIENDLY ○ GLUTEN FREE ● LOW CAL ○ QUICK ● FREEZABLE

THAI SLOW-ROASTED PUMPKIN

We've pumped up pumpkin soup with Thai red curry paste and a mix of crunchy, fresh and spicy toppings. It's a total flavour bomb!

SERVES 4 **PREP** 30 mins **COOK** 2 hours

1.5kg kent pumpkin, unpeeled, cut into wedges, deseeded, plus extra 800g peeled, deseeded, cut into 2cm pieces
80ml (⅓ cup) olive oil
Vegetable oil, to shallow-fry
12 wonton wrappers, cut into 1cm-thick slices
1 brown onion, finely chopped
1 tbs red curry paste
1L (4 cups) chicken stock
60ml (¼ cup) coconut cream, plus extra, to drizzle
2 broccolini stalks, trimmed, halved lengthways, blanched
Coriander drizzle, to serve (see tip)
Finely shredded red cabbage, sliced fresh red chilli, fried shallots, black sesame seeds and lime wedges, to serve

1 Preheat oven to 160°C/140°C fan forced. Line 2 baking trays with baking paper. Place pumpkin wedges on a prepared tray and pumpkin pieces on the other. Drizzle with 60ml (¼ cup) olive oil. Season. Roast wedges for 1½ hours, adding pieces in the last 30 minutes of cooking, or until tender.

2 Fill a saucepan 2cm-deep with vegetable oil. Heat over medium heat. Shallow-fry wonton strips, in batches, for 3-4 minutes or until golden and crisp. Drain on paper towel.

3 Remove wedges from oven. Increase temperature to 200°C/180°C fan forced. Roast pieces for a further 20 minutes or until golden.

4 Meanwhile, scoop flesh from wedges into a bowl. Discard skin. Heat remaining olive oil in a large saucepan over medium heat. Cook onion, stirring, for 5 minutes or until softened. Stir in curry paste for 1 minute or until aromatic. Add stock. Bring to the boil. Stir in pumpkin flesh. Reduce heat to low. Simmer for 15 minutes or until thickened slightly.

5 Use a stick blender to blend soup in pan until smooth. Stir in coconut cream. Warm through over low heat. Ladle soup into serving bowls. Top with extra coconut cream, the drizzle, pumpkin, broccolini, cabbage, chilli, fried shallots, sesame seeds and wonton crisps. Serve with lime wedges.

COOK'S TIP

To make coriander drizzle, use a stick blender to blend ½ cup fresh coriander leaves, 30g baby spinach and 80ml (⅓ cup) olive oil in a bowl until combined. Strain through a fine sieve into a jug. Discard solids. If you like, you can swap this for some pesto.

NUTRITION (PER SERVE)

CALS	FAT	SAT FAT	PROTEIN	CARBS
713	58g	12g	7g	35g

● EASY ● FAMILY-FRIENDLY ○ GLUTEN FREE ○ LOW CAL ○ QUICK ● FREEZABLE

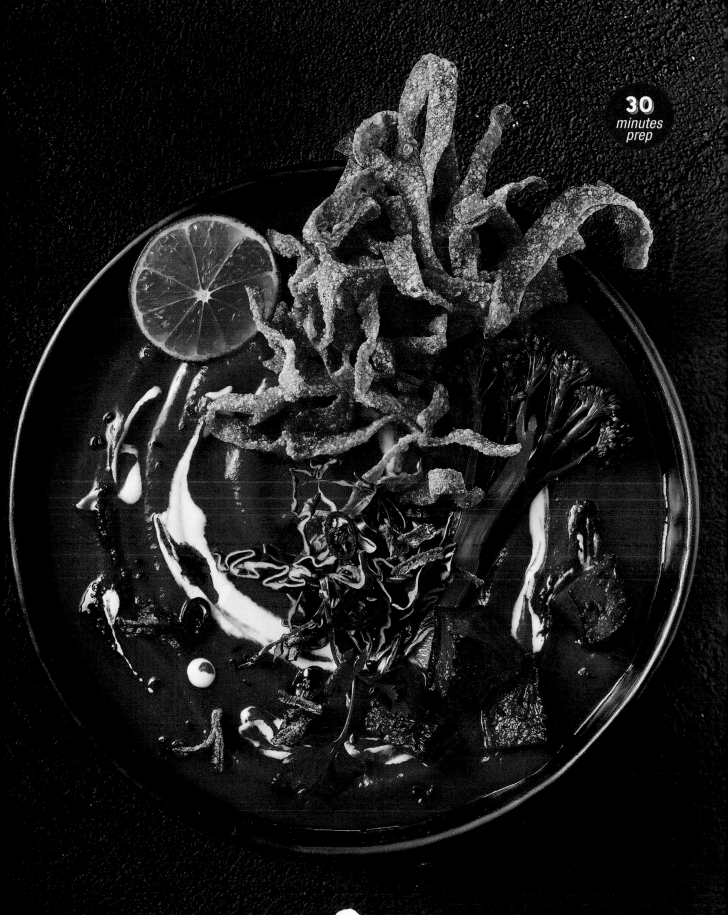

IMMUNITY BOOSTERS

KEEP AT YOUR HEALTHY BEST WITH THE HELP OF SOUPS LADEN WITH FRESH VEG AND ANTIOXIDANTS.

SLOW BARLEY, MISO & GINGER

This slow-cooked barley soup has anti-inflammatory ginger and miso paste for a delicious umami flavour. Even better, there's minimal prep required.

SERVES 4   **PREP** 15 mins   **COOK** 1 hour

2 tsp macadamia oil
1 large onion, finely chopped
3 celery sticks, trimmed, chopped
2 carrots, peeled, chopped
1 tbs finely grated fresh ginger
3 garlic cloves, thinly sliced
110g (½ cup) pearl barley,
    rinsed, drained
1½ tbs miso paste
1.25L (5 cups) vegetable stock
400g frozen podded
    edamame, thawed
1 bunch broccolini, trimmed,
    cut into 3cm lengths
1 tsp tamari
Chopped fresh chives, to serve

1 Heat the oil in a large saucepan over medium heat. Add the onion, celery and carrot. Cook, stirring, for 6-7 minutes or until softened. Add ginger and garlic. Cook, stirring, for 1 minute or until aromatic. Stir in the barley.

2 Stir miso paste and stock into the pan. Bring to the boil. Reduce heat to low, cover and simmer for 45 minutes.

3 Add the edamame and broccolini. Simmer, uncovered, for 5 minutes or until the vegetables are just tender. Stir through the tamari. Season. Serve sprinkles with chives.

NUTRITION (PER SERVE)

CALS	FAT	SAT FAT	PROTEIN	CARBS
207.6	4g	1g	6.3g	29.4g

COOK'S TIP

Miso paste is made from fermented soy beans and has many healthy qualities. You will find it in the Asian food section of the supermarket.

★★★★★ *Healthy. It was the first time we tried edamame and it was a good source of protein.* **MONICA**

● EASY   ● FAMILY-FRIENDLY   ○ GLUTEN FREE   ● LOW CAL   ○ QUICK   ● FREEZABLE

15 minutes prep

FLU-FIGHTER CHICKEN
TURMERIC

Beat the winter sniffles with this hearty chicken soup packed with immune strengthening garlic, chilli, turmeric and sweet potato noodles.

SERVES 4 **PREP** 15 mins **COOK** 2 hours

1.5kg whole chicken
1 small garlic bulb, sliced horizontally, plus extra 3 cloves, finely chopped
5cm-piece fresh ginger, peeled, chopped, plus extra 1 tbs finely chopped
1 tsp white peppercorns
1 tbs coconut oil or olive oil
1 long fresh red chilli, deseeded, finely chopped
2 tsp ground turmeric
270ml can coconut milk
200g pkt fresh sweet potato noodles (see tip)
1-2 tbs tamari, to taste
1 lime, juiced, plus extra wedges, to serve
Fresh coriander sprigs and shredded kaffir lime leaves (optional), to serve

1 Place the chicken in a large saucepan. Add 4L water to cover. Bring to the boil over high heat, skimming any excess fat from surface. Reduce heat to low. Add garlic, ginger and peppercorns. Simmer, skimming occasionally, for 1½ hours or until chicken is very tender. Transfer chicken to a plate, reserving liquid. Cool chicken slightly then coarsely shred the meat, discarding the skin and bones. Strain the reserved stock, discarding the solids.

2 Heat the oil in a large saucepan. Add the chilli, extra garlic and extra ginger. Cook, stirring, for 2 minutes or until aromatic. Add the turmeric. Cook, stirring, for 1 minute or until aromatic.

3 Slowly pour in reserved stock. Add coconut milk. Simmer for 20 minutes or until slightly reduced. Add sweet potato and chicken meat. Simmer for 5 minutes or until noodles are tender. Stir in tamari, to taste, and the lime juice. Season.

4 Ladle soup among serving bowls. Sprinkle with coriander and kaffir, if using. Serve with lime wedges.

COOK'S TIP

You can buy spiralised sweet potato at specialty grocers. If you prefer, peel 200g sweet potato into ribbons, then use a knife to cut each piece into thin strips.

NUTRITION (PER SERVE)

CALS	FAT	SAT FAT	PROTEIN	CARBS
598	28.1g	17.8g	74.5g	9.9g

● EASY ● FAMILY-FRIENDLY ● GLUTEN FREE ○ LOW CAL ○ QUICK ○ FREEZABLE

Delicious soup with a little bit of kick to it. **NERBIT**

TURMERIC, LENTIL & LEMON

This healthy vegetarian soup gets its lovely golden colour from turmeric, which contains curcumin, known for its anti-inflammatory properties.

SERVES 4 **PREP** 15 mins **COOK** 45 mins

2 tsp extra virgin olive oil
1 large red onion, finely chopped
3 celery sticks, finely chopped
2 garlic cloves, crushed
1 lemon, rind finely grated, juiced
1 tsp ground turmeric
½ tsp ground cinnamon
½ tsp dried chilli flakes
500ml (2 cups) gluten-free
    vegetable stock
135g (¾ cup) French-style lentils,
    rinsed, drained
2 vine-ripened tomatoes, chopped
150g green beans, trimmed, sliced
100g trimmed kale, chopped
2 tbs chopped fresh coriander
Natural yoghurt, to serve (optional)

1 Heat the oil in a large saucepan over medium heat. Add the onion and celery. Cook, stirring occasionally, for 5 minutes or until softened. Add the garlic, lemon rind, turmeric, cinnamon and chilli flakes. Cook, stirring, for 1 minute or until aromatic.

2 Add stock, lentils, tomato and 750ml (3 cups) water to the pan. Bring to the boil. Reduce heat to low. Partially cover. Simmer for 30 minutes or until lentils are tender.

3 Add the beans and kale to the pan. Stir to combine. Simmer for 3-4 minutes or until the beans are tender-crisp. Stir in the lemon juice and season with pepper. Stir in the coriander just before serving topped with a dollop of yoghurt, if you like.

COOK'S TIP

French-style lentils are smaller than regular lentils and are blue/grey in colour. You'll find them at the supermarket with the dried legumes.

NUTRITION (PER SERVE)

CALS	FAT	SAT FAT	PROTEIN	CARBS
197	4g	1g	12g	24g

★★★★★ *Regular in our family. Made as written and added some shredded chicken for extra protein :-) Yummo!.* **PRUEFIT**

● EASY ● FAMILY-FRIENDLY ● GLUTEN FREE ● LOW CAL ○ QUICK ● FREEZABLE

CARROT & GINGER WITH YOGHURT

Carrots are a great source of vitamin A, which supports your immune system. Add antioxidant-rich ginger and heart-healthy yoghurt, and you're onto a winner.

SERVES 4 **PREP** 15 mins **COOK** 35 mins

1 large brown onion, coarsely chopped
2 garlic cloves, crushed
2 tsp finely grated fresh ginger
2 tsp ground cumin
500g sweet potato, peeled, coarsely chopped
4 large (about 600g) carrots, peeled, coarsely chopped
1 tsp salt-reduced chicken stock powder
130g (½ cup) low-fat natural yoghurt
Chopped fresh chives, to serve

1 Heat a large saucepan over medium heat. Spray with olive oil spray. Add the onion and cook, stirring occasionally, for 5 minutes or until softened. Add the garlic, ginger and cumin. Cook, stirring, for 1-2 minutes or until aromatic.

2 Add the sweet potato, carrot, 1L (4 cups) water and the stock powder to the pan. Stir well to combine. Increase heat to high. Bring to the boil. Cover and reduce heat to low. Cook for 15-20 minutes or until the vegetables are soft. Remove from the heat.

3 Use a stick blender to blend the soup in the pan until smooth. Return to a low heat and stir until heated through. Season with pepper.

4 Ladle soup among serving bowls. Top with yoghurt and chives, to serve.

COOK'S TIP

To freeze, place the soup in an airtight container in the freezer for up to 3 months.

NUTRITION (PER SERVE)

CALS	FAT	SAT FAT	PROTEIN	CARBS
150	1.5g	0g	6.5g	28g

★★★★★ *One the kids love; make it a lot.* **RINN**

● EASY ● FAMILY-FRIENDLY ○ GLUTEN FREE ● LOW CAL ○ QUICK ● FREEZABLE

CHICKEN, CHICKPEA & KALE

They say chicken soup is good for the soul, and this one is no exception!
The added kale, with high levels of vitamin C and folate, helps fight infection.

SERVES 8 **PREP** 20 mins **COOK** 40 mins

120g (⅔ cup) cracked freekeh
2 tsp extra virgin olive oil
2 brown onions, finely chopped
4 celery sticks, finely chopped
4 garlic cloves, crushed
3 tsp ground cumin
½ tsp ground cinnamon
2L (8 cups) chicken stock
800g chicken thigh fillets,
    fat trimmed
2 x 400g cans no-added-salt
    chickpeas, rinsed, drained
400g peeled and deseeded
    kent pumpkin, finely chopped
1 bunch kale, trimmed,
    coarsely chopped
1 tbs lemon juice

1 Cook the freekeh in a saucepan of boiling water for 12 minutes or until al dente. Drain.

2 Meanwhile, heat the oil in a large saucepan over medium heat. Cook the onion and celery, stirring occasionally, for 6 minutes or until softened. Add the garlic, cumin and cinnamon. Cook, stirring, for 1 minute or until aromatic.

3 Add the stock and 500ml (2 cups) water. Bring to the boil. Add the chicken. Reduce heat to low. Simmer gently, partially covered, for 10 minutes or until chicken is cooked through. Use tongs to transfer the chicken to a clean board. Cool for 5 minutes, then thinly slice.

4 Add the chickpeas, pumpkin and freekeh to the stock mixture. Simmer for 15 minutes or until tender. Add the sliced chicken and kale. Cook, stirring, for 1-2 minutes or until the kale is just wilted. Season with pepper. Drizzle with lemon juice, to serve.

COOK'S TIP

Chickpeas and freekeh are also good for your immunity. They are both high in zinc, which helps your immune cells grow and function.

NUTRITION (PER SERVE)

CALS	FAT	SAT FAT	PROTEIN	CARBS
327	11g	2g	30g	23g

● EASY   ○ FAMILY-FRIENDLY   ○ GLUTEN FREE   ● LOW CAL   ○ QUICK   ● FREEZABLE

★★★★★ *Very good flavour combination. First time using freekeh – very nice. Thanks.* **BLUECONNIE**

VEG-LOADED CHICKEN

Slow-cooked vegies, such as vitamin-rich spinach, carrot, celery, sweet potato and zucchini, will keep you feeling on top of your game.

SERVES 6 **PREP** 30 mins **COOK** 6 hours 55 mins

2 tbs olive oil
1 leek, halved, thinly sliced
1 brown onion, finely chopped
2 carrots, peeled, finely chopped
2 celery sticks, sliced
3 garlic cloves, crushed
350g sweet potato, peeled, chopped
2 (about 370g) parsnips,
   peeled, chopped
2 zucchini, chopped
¾ cup fresh continental
   parsley leaves, chopped
2 lemons, rind finely grated, juiced
60g baby spinach
Crusty wholegrain bread,
   to serve (optional)

SOUP BASE
1.8kg whole organic or
   free-range chicken (see tip)
1 brown onion, halved
1 carrot, halved
1 celery stick, halved
2 fresh bay leaves
4 fresh continental parsley sprigs
1 tbs apple cider vinegar
1L (4 cups) chicken stock

1 To make the soup base, place all ingredients in a slow cooker. Pour in enough water to just cover. Cover and cook on Low for 3 hours.

2 Meanwhile, heat the oil in a saucepan over medium-low heat. Add the leek, onion, carrot, celery and garlic. Cook, stirring occasionally, for 10-12 minutes or until softened.

3 Transfer leek mixture to the slow cooker. Cover and cook, for 2½ hours. Add the sweet potato and parsnip. Cook for 30 minutes or until chicken is falling off the bone.

4 Transfer chicken to a tray and use tongs to remove and discard the halved onion, carrot and celery, the bay leaves and parsley sprigs. Shred the chicken, discarding the skin and bones. Cover to keep warm.

5 Add the zucchini and parsley to the slow cooker. Cook for 30-40 minutes or until all the vegetables are tender.

6 Stir in the chicken meat, lemon rind and juice. Season. Cook for 15 minutes. Remove from heat. Stir in the spinach. Serve with bread, if using.

COOK'S TIP

It is worth getting a good-quality organic or free-range chicken for optimal nutrition, but you may use any whole chicken.

NUTRITION (PER SERVE)

CALS	FAT	SAT FAT	PROTEIN	CARBS
378	13g	3g	40g	19.5g

○ EASY   ● FAMILY-FRIENDLY   ○ GLUTEN FREE   ● LOW CAL   ○ QUICK   ● FREEZABLE

CARROT, SPUD &
BEETROOT

Super-healthy beetroot stars in this easy soup. High in iron and vitamin C, eating beetroot can help to battle infection and promote immunity.

SERVES 6 **PREP** 25 mins **COOK** 1 hour 15 mins

1 bunch (4) beetroot
2 tsp olive oil
1 brown onion, chopped
2 large carrots, peeled, chopped
3 celery stalks, chopped
500g desiree potatoes, peeled, chopped
1 bouquet garni (see tip)
1L (4 cups) gluten-free chicken stock
2 tbs sour cream
Chopped fresh chives, to serve

1 Trim beetroot stems and leaves. Peel and chop the beetroot. Heat the oil in a saucepan over medium-high heat. Add the onion, carrot and celery. Cook, stirring, for 5 minutes or until the onion is softened. Add the beetroot, potato, bouquet garni, stock and 250ml (1 cup) water. Bring to the boil. Reduce heat to medium-low. Simmer, partially covered, for 1 hour or until beetroot is tender. Remove from the heat. Remove and discard bouquet garni.

2 Using a stick blender, blend soup in the pan until smooth. Place soup over low heat. Cook, stirring, for 4-5 minutes or until heated through. Ladle the soup among serving bowls. Top with the sour cream and sprinkle with chives. Season and serve.

COOK'S TIP

To make a bouquet garni, make a small bundle of thyme sprigs, continental parsley stalks and 1-2 fresh bay leaves. Tie together with kitchen string for easy retrieval.

NUTRITION (PER SERVE)

CALS	FAT	SAT FAT	PROTEIN	CARBS
144	5g	2g	4g	18g

★★★★★

This recipe was delicious and easy! **ALICIARULES**

● EASY ● FAMILY-FRIENDLY ● GLUTEN FREE ● LOW CAL ○ QUICK ● FREEZABLE

VEGAN SUPER VEG &
BARLEY

Ward off those flu blues with this power soup, showcasing barley which can strengthen the immune system, reducing the chance of cold and flu.

SERVES 6 **PREP** 15 mins **COOK** 1 hour 5 mins

60ml (¼ cup) extra virgin olive oil
1 red onion, finely chopped
1 leek, trimmed, halved lengthways, thinly sliced
1 celery stick, coarsely chopped
1 large carrot, peeled, coarsely chopped
3 garlic cloves, finely chopped
350g sweet potato, peeled, cut into 2cm pieces
220g (1 cup) pearl barley, rinsed
2 fresh bay leaves
2 large fresh rosemary sprigs
1.5L (6 cups) vegetable stock or plant-based chicken stock (see tip)
2 cups torn kale leaves

ALMOND & BASIL PISTOU
60g (⅓ cup) blanched almonds, toasted
1 garlic clove, finely chopped
1½ cups fresh basil leaves
100ml extra virgin olive oil

1 Heat the oil in a large saucepan over high heat. Add the onion. Reduce heat to low. Cook, stirring often, for 5 minutes or until softened. Add the leek, celery, carrot and garlic. Cook, stirring, for 15 minutes or until well softened (but not golden).

2 Increase heat to high. Add sweet potato. Stir to coat. Add the barley, bay leaves, rosemary, stock and 1L (4 cups) water. Bring to the boil. Reduce heat to low. Simmer, stirring occasionally, for 40 minutes or until thickened and barley is tender.

3 Meanwhile, to make pistou, place almonds and garlic in a small food processor. Process until coarsely chopped. Add the basil, a large pinch of salt and half the oil. Process until nearly smooth. Transfer to a bowl. Stir in remaining oil. Cover and set aside.

4 Stir the kale through the soup until just wilted. Season. Ladle the soup among serving bowls and dollop with pistou, to serve.

COOK'S TIP

There are some brands of stock that are called "chicken-style", but are actually vegan – check the label before buying.

NUTRITION (PER SERVE)

CALS	FAT	SAT FAT	PROTEIN	CARBS
493	32g	4.6g	9.7g	36.7g

○ EASY   ● FAMILY-FRIENDLY   ○ GLUTEN FREE   ○ LOW CAL   ○ QUICK   ● FREEZABLE

★★★★★

Yum! Made this soup as I had vegan company coming... The meat-eating husband LOVED it! **AV83**

BLITZED HERB &
TOMATO

This blender soup is ready in 20 minutes flat! A bonus is that tomatoes are high in lycopene, a powerful antioxidant that protects your immune system.

SERVES 4 **PREP** 10 mins **COOK** 10 mins

1kg (about 8) ripe tomatoes, quartered (see tip)
1 small red onion, chopped
2 tsp olive oil
2 garlic cloves
125ml (½ cup) vegetable stock, plus extra, if needed
2 tbs chopped fresh oregano or basil, plus extra, to serve (optional)
2 tbs chopped fresh chives
1 small baguette, thinly sliced
20g (¼ cup) finely grated parmesan

1 Place the tomato and onion in a blender or food processor. Process until smooth. Heat the oil in a saucepan over medium heat. Add the garlic and cook, stirring, for 30 seconds or until aromatic.

2 Pour in the tomato mixture and stock. Cook, stirring occasionally, for 5-7 minutes or until heated through. Stir in the herbs and season.

3 Meanwhile, preheat an oven grill on high. Place the baguette slices on a baking tray and grill for 1 minute or until toasted. Sprinkle with parmesan and grill for 20-30 seconds or until golden.

4 Ladle soup among serving bowls. Scatter with extra herbs. Serve with the cheese toasts.

COOK'S TIP

Choose nicely ripe tomatoes for a sweeter soup. Also, the redder the tomato, the more lycopene it contains.

NUTRITION (PER SERVE)

CALS	FAT	SAT FAT	PROTEIN	CARBS
183	5g	1g	8g	23g

★★★★★ *Fast, easy and devoured by all!* **RILEY**

● EASY ● FAMILY-FRIENDLY ○ GLUTEN FREE ● LOW CAL ● QUICK ● FREEZABLE

INDEX

USE OUR HANDY INDEX FOR ALL OUR RECIPES SORTED INTO A-Z, KEY GUIDES AND MAIN INGREDIENTS.

The Big Book of Soups
ALPHABETICAL INDEX

Looking for a favourite soup? Here's a list of every recipe in this book to make it easier to find the ones you want to slurp again and again.

B

Beef stroganoff soup	144
Black bean & chipotle	206
Blitzed herb & tomato	244
Buckwheat & mushroom	220

C

Carrot & ginger with yoghurt	234
Carrot, spud & beetroot	240
Cauliflower & ham sandwich	58
Chang mai noodle	120
Chicken & vegetable laksa	124
Chicken & veg with chilli drizzle	70
Chicken, bacon & vermicelli	100
Chicken, chickpea & kale	236
Chicken, miso & ginger	110
Chicken noodle cuppa soup	106
Chilli & black bean pulled pork	146
Classic French onion	30
Cream of English spinach	212
Creamy borlotti bean & pasta	194
Creamy broccoli & 3-cheese	168
Creamy cauliflower & kale	180
Creamy chicken & corn	46
Creamy chicken noodle	98
Creamy tortellini minestrone	80
Creamy vegan tomato & ravioli	192
Curried chickpea & lamb	152

F

15-minute chicken & tortellini	60
15-minute savoury pumpkin	44
Five-a-day minestrone	142
Flu-fighter chicken turmeric	230

French-style seafood	28
Fully-loaded pea soup	154

G

Greek lemon chicken	148
Green curry & broccoli	112
Green tea & dumpling	50

H

Healthy chicken noodle	78
Hearty beef borscht	160
Hearty chorizo & potato	42
Hearty French chicken	34
Hearty Greek moussaka	164
Hearty rice & greens	48

I

Indian-spiced lamb & chickpea	140
Indonesian rice & noodle chicken	92
Italian fish & prawn medley	52
Italian meatball & macaroni	126
Italian sausage & lentil	54
Italian stracciatella egg	66

J

Japanese beef & noodle broth	114
Japanese chicken & tofu soba	122
Japanese chicken ramen	108
Japanese salmon noodle curry	96

K

Keto cauliflower & bacon	38

M

Mega-veg minestrone	158

Mexican chicken & corn 166
Mexican mixed bean amigo 170
Moroccan carrot & ginger 210

O

One-pot cheesy lasagne 84
One-pot spaghetti & meatball 82

P

Pancetta & borlotti 132
Pea & smoked ham 176
Pork & bean soupy goulash 174
Pork & sweet corn wonton 116
Potato & leek with chorizo 68
Potato & Swiss cheese 64
Potato, cauliflower & carrot 200
Prawn & salmon chowder 26
Pumpkin curry noodle 94
Pumpkin, haloumi bites
   & croutons 196

Q

Quick Thai red chicken curry 88
Quinoa, feta & broccoli 56

R

Racy Japanese tofu ramen 90
Roast carrot & coriander pesto 190
Roasted tomato & capsicum 218

S

Shredded chicken nabe 40
Slow barley, miso & ginger 228
Slow-cooked beef & barley 130
Slow-cooked freekeh & lamb 134
Slow-cooked red lentil 216
Slow cooker chicken laksa 104

Slow cooker chicken noodle 156
Slow cooker mulligatawny 138
Slow cooker pork belly ramen 86
Slow lamb & barley 162
Slow pho bo beef 172
Smoky chipotle Mex pumpkin 74
Speedy Tuscan tortellini 102
Speedy winter minestrone 198
Spiced cauliflower & tahini 208
Spiced chickpea & quinoa vegie 182
Spicy black bean & corn 188
Spicy Thai pumpkin & prawn 72
Spring vegie with whipped feta 202
Super beetroot & potato 186
Super green coconut 214
Super greens & tofu crouton 62
Super-vegie pumpkin 36
Sweet potato & chickpea 150
Sweet potato & chilli cream 222

T

Thai slow-roasted pumpkin 224
Tomato, fennel & meatball 24
Turmeric, lentil & lemon 232
Tuscan bread soup 136

U

Udon & Peking duck bowl 118
Ultimate vegetarian ramen 184

V

Vegan super-veg & barley 242
Vegetarian Vietnamese pho 204
Veg-loaded chicken 238

Z

Zucchini & borlotti minestrone 32

The Big Book of Soups
INDEX BY KEY GUIDE

Most of our soups are easy to make, but look here for a family-friendly dinner, freezable or gluten-free recipe, a speedy soup or healthier low-cal bowl.

● FAMILY-FRIENDLY

Beef stroganoff soup	144
Blitzed herb & tomato	244
Carrot & ginger with yoghurt	234
Carrot, spud & beetroot	240
Cauliflower & ham sandwich	58
Chicken, bacon & vermicelli	100
Chicken noodle cuppa soup	106
Chilli & black bean pulled pork	146
Creamy borlotti bean & pasta	194
Creamy broccoli & 3-cheese	168
Creamy chicken & corn	46
Creamy tortellini minestrone	80
Creamy vegan tomato & ravioli	192
Curried chickpea & lamb	152
15-minute savoury pumpkin	44
Five-a-day minestrone	142
Flu-fighter chicken turmeric	230
Fully-loaded pea soup	154
Greek lemon chicken	148
Healthy chicken noodle	78
Hearty beef borscht	160
Hearty chorizo & potato	42
Hearty French chicken	34
Hearty Greek moussaka	164
Hearty rice & greens	48
Indian-spiced lamb & chickpea	140
Italian meatball & macaroni	126
Italian sausage & lentil	54
Italian stracciatella egg	66
Japanese chicken ramen	108
Keto cauliflower & bacon	38
Mega-veg minestrone	158
Mexican chicken & corn	166
Mexican mixed bean amigo	170
Moroccan carrot & ginger	210
One-pot cheesy lasagne	84
One-pot spaghetti & meatball	82

Pancetta & borlotti	132
Pea & smoked ham	176
Pork & bean soupy goulash	174
Potato & leek with chorizo	68
Potato & Swiss cheese	64
Potato, cauliflower & carrot	200
Prawn & salmon chowder	26
Pumpkin curry noodle	94
Pumpkin, haloumi bites & croutons	196
Roast carrot & coriander pesto	190
Roasted tomato & capsicum	218
Shredded chicken nabe	40
Slow barley, miso & ginger	228
Slow-cooked beef & barley	130
Slow-cooked freekeh & lamb	134
Slow-cooked red lentil	216
Slow cooker chicken noodle	156
Slow cooker mulligatawny	138
Slow lamb & barley	162
Smoky chipotle Mex pumpkin	74
Speedy Tuscan tortellini	102
Speedy winter minestrone	198
Spiced cauliflower & tahini	208
Spiced chickpea & quinoa vegie	182
Spicy black bean & corn	188
Spring vegie with whipped feta	202
Super beetroot & potato	186
Super greens & tofu crouton	62
Super-vegie pumpkin	36
Sweet potato & chickpea	150
Thai slow-roasted pumpkin	224
Tomato, fennel & meatball	24
Turmeric, lentil & lemon	232
Tuscan bread soup	136
Vegan super-veg & barley	242
Veg-loaded chicken	238
Zucchini & borlotti minestrone	32

● GLUTEN FREE

Black bean & chipotle	206
Buckwheat & mushroom	220
Carrot, spud & beetroot	240
Chicken & veg with chilli drizzle	70
Chicken, bacon & vermicelli	100
Chilli & black bean pulled pork	146
Creamy cauliflower & kale	180
Creamy chicken & corn	46
Creamy chicken noodle	98
15-minute savoury pumpkin	44
Flu-fighter chicken turmeric	230
Greek lemon chicken	148
Green curry & broccoli	112
Healthy chicken noodle	78
Hearty beef borscht	160
Hearty rice & greens	48
Indian-spiced lamb & chickpea	140
Indonesian rice & noodle chicken	92
Italian stracciatella egg	66
Keto cauliflower & bacon	38
Moroccan carrot & ginger	210
Pea & smoked ham	176
Quick Thai red chicken curry	88
Quinoa, feta & broccoli	56
Roast carrot & coriander pesto	190
Slow pho bo beef	172
Spicy black bean & corn	188
Super beetroot & potato	186
Super green coconut	214
Super-vegie pumpkin	36
Sweet potato & chickpea	150
Tomato, fennel & meatball	24
Turmeric, lentil & lemon	232
Vegetarian Vietnamese pho	204
Zucchini & borlotti minestrone	32

● LOW CAL

Black bean & chipotle	206
Blitzed herb & tomato	244
Buckwheat & mushroom	220
Carrot & ginger with yoghurt	234
Carrot, spud & beetroot	240
Chicken & veg with chilli drizzle	70
Chicken, chickpea & kale	236
Chicken noodle cuppa soup	106
Creamy broccoli & 3-cheese	168
Creamy cauliflower & kale	180
Creamy chicken & corn	46
Creamy chicken noodle	98
Creamy vegan tomato & ravioli	192
15-minute chicken & tortellini	60
15-minute savoury pumpkin	44
Five-a-day minestrone	142
Greek lemon chicken	148
Green curry & broccoli	112
Green tea & dumpling	50
Healthy chicken noodle	78
Hearty beef borscht	160
Hearty chorizo & potato	42
Hearty rice & greens	48
Indian-spiced lamb & chickpea	140
Italian fish & prawn medley	52
Italian meatball & macaroni	126
Italian stracciatella egg	66
Japanese chicken & tofu soba	122
Mexican chicken & corn	166
Moroccan carrot & ginger	210
Pancetta & borlotti	132
Pork & sweet corn wonton	116
Potato & leek with chorizo	68
Potato, cauliflower & carrot	200
Quinoa, feta & broccoli	56
Racy Japanese tofu ramen	90
Shredded chicken nabe	40
Slow barley, miso & ginger	228
Slow-cooked beef & barley	130
Slow-cooked freekeh & lamb	134
Slow cooker chicken noodle	156
Slow cooker mulligatawny	138
Slow pho bo beef	172
Spiced chickpea & quinoa vegie	182
Spicy black bean & corn	188
Spring vegie with whipped feta	202
Super beetroot & potato	186
Super green coconut	214
Super greens & tofu crouton	62
Super-vegie pumpkin	36
Sweet potato & chickpea	150
Sweet potato & chilli cream	222
Tomato, fennel & meatball	24
Turmeric, lentil & lemon	232
Tuscan bread soup	136
Udon & Peking duck bowl	118
Ultimate vegetarian ramen	184
Vegetarian Vietnamese pho	204
Veg-loaded chicken	238

● QUICK

Blitzed herb & tomato	244
Cauliflower & ham sandwich	58
Chang mai noodle	120
Chicken & vegetable laksa	124
Chicken, bacon & vermicelli	100
Chicken, miso & ginger	110
Chicken noodle cuppa soup	106
15-minute chicken & tortellini	60
15-minute savoury pumpkin	44
French-style seafood	28
Green tea & dumpling	50
Hearty rice & greens	48
Italian stracciatella egg	66
Japanese beef & noodle broth	114
Japanese chicken ramen	108
Japanese salmon noodle curry	96
Prawn & salmon chowder	26
Quick Thai red chicken curry	88
Racy Japanese tofu ramen	90
Slow cooker chicken laksa	104
Speedy Tuscan tortellini	102
Speedy winter minestrone	198
Spring vegie with whipped feta	202
Super green coconut	214
Super greens & tofu crouton	62
Udon & Peking duck bowl	118

● FREEZABLE

Black bean & chipotle	206
Blitzed herb & tomato	244
Carrot & ginger with yoghurt	234
Carrot, spud & beetroot	240
Cauliflower & ham sandwich	58
Chicken, chickpea & kale	236
Cream of English spinach	212
Creamy borlotti bean & pasta	194
Creamy broccoli & 3-cheese	168
Creamy cauliflower & kale	180
Creamy vegan tomato & ravioli	192
15-minute savoury pumpkin	44
Five-a-day minestrone	142
Fully-loaded pea soup	154
Hearty beef borscht	160
Hearty chorizo & potato	42
Hearty Greek Moussaka	164
Indian-spiced lamb & chickpea	140
Italian sausage & lentil	54
Keto cauliflower & bacon	38
Mexican mixed bean amigo	170
Moroccan carrot & ginger	210
Pancetta & borlotti	132
Pea & smoked ham	176
Pork & bean soupy goulash	174
Potato & leek with chorizo	68
Potato & Swiss cheese	64
Potato, cauliflower & carrot	200
Pumpkin, haloumi bites & croutons	196
Quinoa, feta & broccoli	56
Roast carrot & coriander pesto	190
Roasted tomato & capsicum	218
Slow barley, miso & ginger	228
Slow-cooked freekeh & lamb	134
Slow-cooked red lentil	216
Slow cooker mulligatawny	138
Slow lamb & barley	162
Smoky chipotle Mex pumpkin	74
Spiced cauliflower & tahini	208
Spiced chickpea & quinoa vegie	182
Spicy black bean & corn	188
Super beetroot & potato	186
Super green coconut	214
Super greens & tofu crouton	62
Super-vegie pumpkin	36
Sweet potato & chickpea	150
Sweet potato & chilli cream	222
Thai slow-roasted pumpkin	224
Tomato, fennel & meatball	24
Turmeric, lentil & lemon	232
Tuscan bread soup	136
Vegan super-veg & barley	242
Vegetarian Vietnamese pho	204
Veg-loaded chicken	238
Zucchini & borlotti minestrone	32

The Big Book of Soups
INDEX BY MAIN INGREDIENT

Check out our list of star soup ingredients to find your main protein or seasonal vegie preference – it will make shopping and cooking easier.

ASIAN GREENS

Creamy chicken noodle	98
Japanese beef & noodle broth	114
Japanese chicken & tofu soba	122
Japanese salmon noodle curry	96
Racy Japanese tofu ramen	90
Shredded chicken nabe	40
Udon & Peking duck bowl	118
Ultimate vegetarian ramen	184
Vegetarian Vietnamese pho	204

BEEF & LAMB

Beef stroganoff soup	144
Curried chickpea & lamb	152
One-pot cheesy lasagne	84
One-pot spaghetti & meatball	82
Hearty beef borscht	160
Hearty Greek moussaka	164
Indian-spiced lamb & chickpea	140
Italian meatball & macaroni	126
Japanese beef & noodle broth	114
Slow-cooked beef & barley	130
Slow-cooked freekeh & lamb	134
Slow lamb & barley	162
Slow pho bo beef	172
Speedy Tuscan tortellini	102

BROCCOLI(NI)

Chicken & vegetable laksa	124
Chicken, miso & ginger	110
Creamy broccoli & 3-cheese	168
15-minute chicken & tortellini	60
Green curry & broccoli	112

Green tea & dumpling	50
Italian meatball & macaroni	126
Quinoa, feta & broccoli	56
Slow barley, miso & ginger	228
Super greens & tofu crouton	62

CAULIFLOWER

Cauliflower & ham sandwich	58
Creamy cauliflower & kale	180
Keto cauliflower & bacon	38
Potato, cauliflower & carrot	200
Spiced cauliflower & tahini	208
Spiced chickpea & quinoa vegie	182

CHICKEN

Chang mai noodle	120
Chicken & vegetable laksa	124
Chicken & veg with chilli drizzle	70
Chicken, bacon & vermicelli	100
Chicken, chickpea & kale	236
Chicken, miso & ginger	110
Chicken noodle cuppa soup	106
Creamy chicken & corn	46
Creamy chicken noodle	98
15-minute chicken & tortellini	60
Flu-fighter chicken turmeric	230
Greek lemon chicken	148
Healthy chicken noodle	78
Hearty French chicken	34
Indonesian rice & noodle chicken	92
Italian stracciatella egg	66
Japanese chicken & tofu soba	122
Japanese chicken ramen	108

Mexican chicken & corn	166
Quick Thai red chicken curry	88
Shredded chicken nabe	40
Slow cooker chicken laksa	104
Slow cooker chicken noodle	156
Slow cooker mulligatawny	138
Veg-loaded chicken	238

CORN

Black bean & chipotle	206
Chicken noodle cuppa soup	106
Creamy chicken & corn	46
Hearty chorizo & potato	42
Pork & sweet corn wonton	116
Prawn & salmon chowder	26
Quick Thai red chicken curry	88
Mexican chicken & corn	166
Mexican mixed bean amigo	17
Spicy black bean & corn	188

LEGUMES
(BEANS, PEAS, LENTILS)

Black bean & chipotle	206
Chicken, bacon & vermicelli	100
Chicken, chickpea & kale	236
Chilli & black bean pulled pork	146
Creamy borlotti bean & pasta	194
Creamy tortellini minestrone	80
Curried chickpea & lamb	152
Five-a-day minestrone	142
Fully-loaded pea soup	154
Green tea & dumpling	50
Hearty Greek moussaka	164

Indian-spiced lamb & chickpea 140
Italian fish & prawn medley 52
Italian sausage & lentil 54
Japanese chicken ramen 108
Mega-veg minestrone 158
Mexican chicken & corn 166
Mexican mixed bean amigo 170
Moroccan carrot & ginger 210
Pancetta & borlotti 132
Pea & smoked ham 176
Pork & bean soupy goulash 174
Potato & leek with chorizo 68
Slow barley, miso & ginger 228
Slow-cooked red lentil 216
Slow cooker mulligatawny 138
Smoky chipotle Mex pumpkin 74
Speedy Tuscan tortellini 102
Speedy winter minestrone 198
Spiced chickpea & quinoa vegie 182
Spicy black bean & corn 188
Spring vegie with whipped feta 202
Super green coconut 214
Sweet potato & chickpea 150
Turmeric, lentil & lemon 232
Tuscan bread soup 136
Zucchini & borlotti minestrone 32

PORK
(+HAM, BACON & CHORIZO)
Cauliflower & ham sandwich 58
Chicken, bacon & vermicelli 100
Chilli & black bean pulled pork 146
Creamy tortellini minestrone 80
Creamy vegan tomato & ravioli 192
Five-a-day minestrone 142
Fully-loaded pea soup 154
Hearty chorizo & potato 42
Italian sausage & lentil 54
Keto cauliflower & bacon 38
Pancetta & borlotti 132
Pea & smoked ham 176
Pork & bean soupy goulash 174
Pork & sweet corn wonton 116
Potato & leek with chorizo 68

Potato & Swiss cheese 64
Slow cooker pork belly ramen 86
Super-vegie pumpkin 36
Tomato, fennel & meatball 24
Tuscan bread soup 136
Zucchini & borlotti minestrone 32

POTATO
(+SWEET POTATO)
Carrot & ginger with yoghurt 234
Carrot, spud & beetroot 240
Cauliflower & ham sandwich 58
Chicken & veg with chilli drizzle 70
Cream of English spinach 212
Creamy broccoli & three-cheese 168
Creamy chicken noodle 98
Curried chickpea & lamb 152
Flu-fighter chicken turmeric 230
Green curry & broccoli 112
Hearty beef borscht 160
Hearty chorizo & potato 42
Hearty French chicken 34
Potato & leek with chorizo 68
Potato & Swiss cheese 64
Potato, cauliflower & carrot 200
Quinoa, feta & broccoli 56
Speedy winter minestrone 198
Spiced cauliflower & tahini 208
Spicy black bean & corn 188
Super beetroot & potato 186
Super-vegie pumpkin 36
Sweet potato & chickpea 150
Sweet potato & chilli cream 222
Tuscan bread soup 136
Vegan super-veg & barley 242
Veg-loaded chicken 238
Zucchini & borlotti minestrone 32

PUMPKIN
Chicken, chickpea & kale 236
15-minute savoury pumpkin 44
Pumpkin curry noodle 94
Pumpkin, haloumi bites & croutons 196

Smoky chipotle Mex pumpkin 74
Spiced chickpea & quinoa vegie 182
Spicy Thai pumpkin & prawn 72
Super-vegie pumpkin 36
Thai slow-roasted pumpkin 224
Ultimate vegetarian ramen 184

SEAFOOD
French-style seafood 28
Green tea & dumpling 50
Italian fish & prawn medley 52
Japanese salmon noodle curry 96
Prawn & salmon chowder 26
Spicy Thai pumpkin & prawn 72

SPINACH, KALE
Chicken, chickpea & kale 236
Cream of English spinach 212
Creamy cauliflower & kale 180
Creamy tortellini minestrone 80
Creamy vegan tomato & ravioli 192
15-minute chicken & tortellini 60
Hearty rice & greens 48
Italian sausage & lentil 54
Italian stracciatella egg 66
Slow cooker pork belly ramen 86
Super green coconut 214
Super greens & tofu crouton 62
Turmeric, lentil & lemon 232

TOFU
Japanese chicken & tofu soba 122
Racy Japanese tofu ramen 90
Super greens & tofu crouton 62
Vegetarian Vietnamese pho 204

CREDITS

editor-in-chief Brodee Myers
executive editor Dani Bertollo
food director Michelle Southan
creative director Giota Letsios
book art director Natasha Barisa
book subeditor Natasha Shaw
book food editor Tracy Rutherford
nutrition editor Chrissy Freer
editorial coordinator Bonnie Moorhouse

managing director – food and travel Fiona Nilsson

HarperCollins*Publishers* Australia
publishing director Brigitta Doyle
head of Australian non-fiction Helen Littleton
managing editor adult books Belinda Yuille

CONTRIBUTORS

Recipes

Alison Adams, Charlotte Binns-McDonald, Claire Brookman, Lucy Busuttil, Kim Coverdale, Amber de Florio, Chrissy Freer, Amira Georgy, Louise Keats, Cathie Lonnie, Gemma Luongo, Liz Macri, Lucy Nunes, Louise Patniotis, Miranda Payne, Matt Preston, Kerrie Ray, Tracy Rutherford, Michelle Southan, Jo-Anne Woodman, Katrina Woodman

Photography

Guy Bailey, Steve Brown, Julie Crespel, Vanessa Levis, Nigel Lough, Mark O'Meara, Al Richardson, Jeremy Simons, Brett Stevens, Craig Wall, Andrew Young

HarperCollins*Publishers*

Australia • Brazil • Canada • France • Germany • Holland
• Hungary • India • Italy • Japan • Mexico • New Zealand
• Poland • Spain • Sweden • Switzerland • United Kingdom
• United States of America

First published in Australia in 2022
by HarperCollins*Publishers* Australia Pty Limited
ABN 36 009 913 517
harpercollins.com.au

A catalogue record for this book is available
from the National Library of Australia

ISBN 978 1 4607 6219 6 (paperback)

Colour reproduction by Splitting Image Colour Studio,
Clayton Victoria
Printed and bound in China by RR Donnelley

8 7 6 5 4 3 2 1   22 23 24

THANK YOU

At taste.com.au HQ, we love creating easy and delicious meals! *The Big Book of Soups* is a cookbook that will give you all the ideas and know-how you need to create sensational bowls of nutritious soup all year round. We'd like to thank everyone on the Taste team who contributed to this book – from our foodies to photographers, stylists, designers, subeditors and the digital team. Each recipe is a result of amazing passion and teamwork.

A huge thank you as well to Brigitta Doyle and Helen Littleton, our partners at HarperCollins. We're very thankful for your expertise and support.

We'd also like to thank ... you, the audience of taste.com.au! Thousands of passionate cooks visit our site every day to plan, cook and share their reviews, ratings and recipe twists and tips. We love hearing about your passion for cooking and the gusto with which you make our recipes, so keep those reviews, comments and photos coming. And continue to slurp soup!